The Complete DISCARD *Guide to*

ORGANIC
LAWN CARE

*Everything You Need to Know
Explained Simply*

Sandy Baker

THE COMPLETE GUIDE TO ORGANIC LAWN CARE: EVERYTHING YOU NEED TO KNOW EXPLAINED SIMPLY

Baker, Sandy Ann, 1976-
The complete guide to organic lawn care : everything you need to know explained simply / by: Sandy Baker.
   p. cm.
Includes bibliographical references and index.
ISBN-13: 978-1-60138-367-9 (alk. paper)
ISBN-10: 1-60138-367-3 (alk. paper)
1. Lawns. 2. Organic gardening. I. Title.
SB433.B135 2011
635'.0484--dc22

2011000500

LIMIT OF LIABILITY/DISCLAIMER OF WARRANTY: The publisher and the author make no representations or warranties with respect to the accuracy or completeness of the contents of this work and specifically disclaim all warranties, including without limitation warranties of fitness for a particular purpose. No warranty may be created or extended by sales or promotional materials. The advice and strategies contained herein may not be suitable for every situation. This work is sold with the understanding that the publisher is not engaged in rendering legal, accounting, or other professional services. If professional assistance is required, the services of a competent professional should be sought. Neither the publisher nor the author shall be liable for damages arising herefrom. The fact that an organization or website is referred to in this work as a citation and/or a potential source of further information does not mean that the author or the publisher endorses the information the organization or website may provide or recommendations it may make. Further, readers should be aware that Internet websites listed in this work may have changed or disappeared between when this work was written and when it is read.

TRADEMARK DISCLAIMER: All trademarks, trade names, or logos mentioned or used are the property of their respective owners and are used only to directly describe the products being provided. Every effort has been made to properly capitalize, punctuate, identify, and attribute trademarks and trade names to their respective owners, including the use of ® and ™ wherever possible and practical. Atlantic Publishing Group, Inc. is not a partner, affiliate, or licensee with the holders of said trademarks.

Printed in the United States

PROJECT MANAGER: Amy Moczynski • AMoczynski@atlantic-pub.com
INTERIOR LAYOUT: Antoinette D'Amore • addesign@videotron.ca
PROOFREADER: Gretchen Pressley • phygem@gmail.com
COVER DESIGN: Meg Buchner • meg@megbuchner.com
BACK COVER DESIGN: Jackie Miller • millerjackiej@gmail.com

Printed on Recycled Paper

We recently lost our beloved pet "Bear," who was not only our best and dearest friend but also the "Vice President of Sunshine" here at Atlantic Publishing. He did not receive a salary but worked tirelessly 24 hours a day to please his parents. Bear was a rescue dog that turned around and showered myself, my wife, Sherri, his grandparents Jean, Bob, and Nancy, and every person and animal he met (maybe not rabbits) with friendship and love. He made a lot of people smile every day.

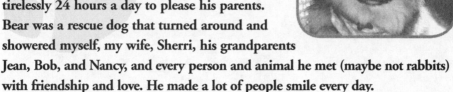

We wanted you to know that a portion of the profits of this book will be donated to The Humane Society of the United States. *–Douglas & Sherri Brown*

The human-animal bond is as old as human history. We cherish our animal companions for their unconditional affection and acceptance. We feel a thrill when we glimpse wild creatures in their natural habitat or in our own backyard.

Unfortunately, the human-animal bond has at times been weakened. Humans have exploited some animal species to the point of extinction.

The Humane Society of the United States makes a difference in the lives of animals here at home and worldwide. The HSUS is dedicated to creating a world where our relationship with animals is guided by compassion. We seek a truly humane society in which animals are respected for their intrinsic value and where the human-animal bond is strong.

Want to help animals? We have plenty of suggestions. Adopt a pet from a local shelter, join The Humane Society and be a part of our work to help companion animals and wildlife. You will be funding our educational, legislative, investigative and outreach projects in the U.S. and across the globe.

Or perhaps you'd like to make a memorial donation in honor of a pet, friend or relative? You can through our Kindred Spirits program. And if you'd like to contribute in a more structured way, our Planned Giving Office has suggestions about estate planning, annuities, and even gifts of stock that avoid capital gains taxes.

Maybe you have land you would like to preserve as a lasting habitat for wildlife. Our Wildlife Land Trust can help you. Perhaps the land you want to share is a backyard — that's enough. Our Urban Wildlife Sanctuary Program will show you how to create a habitat for your wild neighbors.

So you see, it's easy to help animals. And The HSUS is here to help.

THE HUMANE SOCIETY
OF THE UNITED STATES.

2100 L Street NW • Washington, DC 20037 • 202-452-1100
www.hsus.org

Acknowledgement

I would like to thank all of those who worked hard to make this book happen, including Douglas Brown and Amy Moczynski, who both worked with me to complete this guide. In addition, I would like to thank my family and friends for their support and encouragement throughout the process.

Dedication

I dedicate this book to my patient husband, Owen, and to my three kids,
Christin, Andrew, and Matthew, whom I cherish.

Table of Contents

Chapter 8: Transitioning a Lawn to Organic 165

Chapter 9: Water and the Natural Lawn ..195

Chapter 10: Getting Control of Weeds and Pests 223

Chapter 11: Mowing Your Lawn The Right Way..................................245

Chapter 12: Going for Less Lawn..............257

Conclusion 263

Appendix A: Commercial Organic Herbicides..................................265

THE TIME IS RIGHT FOR ORGANIC LAWN CARE

*I*f you have made the decision to cut back on the use of chemical fertilizers, pesticides, and weed killers on your home's lawn because of the harm they may cause not only to the environment but also to your family and pets, then you are among a fast-growing number of Americans concerned enough to do something about it. Surveys conducted by the National Gardening Association (NGA) revealed that as many as 12 million households were applying "natural" products exclusively to their lawns and gardens in 2008, a whopping 42 percent increase from the 5 million homes reported in 2004. The NGA suggests that this number could rise to as many as 17 million in the coming years as more Americans begin using environmentally friendly methods on their lawns and gardens. The time is right to start thinking seriously about what you can do in your own backyard to have a positive, global impact on the health of our planet and all of its inhabitants.

You may want to make this transition but are unsure of where to begin. This book will show you step by step how to create a beautiful and healthy lawn. After reading this book, you will have all of the information you need to do as little or as much as you can take on, whether you decide to take a few simple but critical steps to improve the health of your lawn or create an organic lawn from scratch.

Using the environmentally friendly lawn care methods and products that support the soil and surrounding environment are necessary to create and maintain a healthy, beautiful lawn. Organic lawn care is often about what *not* to apply to a lawn. Slightly altering your routine can result in profound results and require less effort than your previous lawn care regime.

However you decide to proceed, this book will be your companion along the way, guiding you from first step to the last as you do your part to create a safe haven for your family and help make Earth a healthy place to live.

About This Book

Making the transition from a synthetic lawn to a natural or organic lawn may appear at first glance to be an overwhelming undertaking. To help ease the way, this book has been carefully organized to make the process understandable and achievable.

Chapters 1 through 4 explain why organic lawn care is so critical, including the essential ingredients for any organic lawn. With this information in hand, you will be guided through the steps you need to take to not only convert your synthetic lawn to an organic one, which is discussed in Chapters 5 through 8, but also to maintain it without resorting to toxic chemicals or outmoded lawn care methods that can damage your lawn, which is discussed in Chapters 9 through 12. Finally, supplemental resources and a bibliography are included at the end of the book to provide you with additional information on organic lawn care that you may find helpful.

How to Use This Book

It is recommended that you read the first four chapters, which serve as a foundation for the rest of the book and will help you understand why you are doing what you are doing. Then, select the chapter (5, 6, or 7) that best represents the option you have chosen to create your organic lawn. Make sure to read it in its entirety before you begin the actual work.

The detailed table of contents and index will help you find information quickly, making this book an excellent reference that you will return to again and again.

Chapter 1

WHAT IS ORGANIC LAWN CARE?

*I*t is important to begin by defining all of the terms associated with organic lawn care so you understand exactly how to use the terms in this specific context. Each term — "organic," "lawn," and "care" — may mean different things to different people in different situations. It is important to clarify what these terms mean to prevent any confusion.

The term **organic** means any natural substance derived from an animal, plant, or mineral source. The opposite of organic or natural would be synthetic or artificial, which refers to any substance produced in a laboratory using some form of human intervention. This distinction is important to note because a lawn, by its very nature, is an artificial creation that cannot exist without human intervention. But, in the case of organic lawn care, human intervention is used to create an environment that mimics a natural environment as much as possible and focuses on the long-term health of the lawn and its surroundings, often at the expense of such short-term rewards as uniformly and intensely green or fast-growing grass.

Another important distinction to note is organic or natural does not necessarily mean nontoxic. **Nontoxic** refers to substances safe to touch with bare hands that will not harm the body of a human or animal. Many naturally occurring substances are dangerous, such as poison ivy and coral snake venom. You may end up using natural yet toxic substances for various reasons as you practice environmentally friendly lawn care.

The primary difference between natural and artificial substances is that though the toxic qualities of some natural substances can be harmful in the short term, they are quite beneficial to the lawn and surrounding environment in the long term. The poisonous nature of artificial substances is often harmful in the short and long term and represents one of the main reasons many homeowners avoid using these chemicals on their plants.

A **lawn** is an area of land that has grass growing on it and that a person mows on a regular basis. The words "turf" and "green" often mean the same thing. A **field**, on the other hand, is an area containing plants that is not mowed on a regular basis. This book will focus on lawns that commonly surround single-family homes for recreational use or for aesthetic appeal.

Organic lawn care, then, is the practice of creating and maintaining the health and well-being of a lawn using natural or organic — as opposed to artificial or synthetic — substances and methods that promote the long-term health of the lawn's soil and grass and the surrounding environment.

Brief History of Organic Lawn Care

Organic lawn care began as early as 4,000 B.C. when domesticated animals, such as sheep, horses, and cattle, grazed near people's farms and homes and kept the grass from growing too tall. These animals were not used specifically to create lawns as people know them today; instead, the land provided a source of food for livestock. People also used simple cutting tools, such as scythes and sickles, to maintain low-cut areas of grass around their homes.

Wealthy aristocrats in Europe as early as the 17th century surrounded their palatial homes with beautiful lawns and gardens. They did not have access to chemical fertilizers and pesticides, but they could afford to employ the massive workforce needed to maintain these showpieces of horticultural magnificence. It was not until 1830 when Edwin Budding invented the first lawn mower in England that lawn care was accomplished with machines.

The American lawn of today's homeowner came into existence as a result of the growth of the post-World War II suburb. The introduction of the garden hose, the rotary lawn mower, and weed-free grass seeds made lawn maintenance an easy proposition. By the 1940s, companies began introducing chemical fertilizers as a means of artificially stimulating grass growth, and companies created pesticides to eliminate weeds and bugs.

A growing movement promoting organic gardening began in 1942 with the publication of J. I. Rodale's magazine, *Organic Farming*. The articles educated the masses about the dangers of chemical fertilizers and pesticides and the benefits of gardening in cooperation with Mother Nature. It was not long before these ideas spread into the arena of lawn care, and consumers began demanding safe products for use on their lawns as early as the 1980s.

Organic lawn care is not a new idea; it is a return to the natural way of creating a beautiful lawn that maintains a soil's vitality and integrity and keeps the environment safe. People's ancestors practiced this form of lawn care out of necessity because they did not have access to the chemicals and machinery available on the market today. Consumers disdained the use of these natural methods in their mad rush to create overnight lawns resembling golf courses, but these quick-fix methods had detrimental consequences the planet still faces today.

Problems with Traditional Lawn Care

Traditional lawn care creates a host of problems many homeowners either have not been aware of or perhaps have ignored because of the limited amount of time they have to devote to lawn maintenance. Traditional methods:

- Result in weaker grass and unhealthy soil

- Are toxic to family and pets

- Are toxic to the environment

- Are often more expensive to implement

Weak grass and unhealthy soil

When you use an artificial fertilizer on a lawn, it unnaturally boosts the levels of nitrogen and other nutrients grass needs to grow. The typical way plants and grass get the nutrients they need is from the soil through their root systems. Synthetic fertilizers do not add nutrients to the soil. Instead they are immediately sucked into the plant. Although the blades of grass do grow faster and are more plentiful, artificially fertilizing also creates four problems:

- Grass blades are weaker.

- The root system does not grow deeply enough.

- The grass is far more susceptible to disease.

- The soil becomes overly acidic or salty because it is too quickly depleted of nutrients.

The primary culprit is the nitrogen the fertilizer offers. Excess nitrogen consumption is a trait built into grass as a survival mechanism. These fertilizers are so successful because the grass already has a natural tendency to overuse nitrogen, even if it does not need it.

However, giving the grass access to extra nitrogen leads to nitrogen addiction. Because of the resulting rapid growth, many homeowners mow their lawns even lower, leaving the grass with blades too short to gain sufficient energy from the sun. Grass that consumes too much nitrogen is not more colorful because it is healthier; instead, it is producing more chlorophyll — the green stuff that enables plants to draw energy from sunlight — to compensate for the fact that it does not get enough sun.

A healthy balance in any system requires maintenance, and grass is no exception. For example, when there is too much nitrogen in the soil, grass needs more water to compensate. The excess water causes other imbalances, though. The grass's roots, which serve to anchor a plant in the soil and ensure its survival during drought, do not extend deeply enough into the soil and do not grow with the same vigor. Deep root growth occurs when the roots have to dig down into the soil to find water. Even with heavy watering to saturate the lower levels of soil, the roots will not grow deeply enough because water is available closer to the surface. This vicious cycle continues as one imbalance perpetuates another and another.

Instead of using fertilizer to increase nitrogen levels to stimulate "healthy" plant growth, a better solution would be to test the soil to determine which nutrients are in short supply and add those instead of overloading the plant with nitrogen, a popular fix in traditional lawn care. *See Chapter 2 for information on soil testing.*

Although fertilizers produce a faster-growing and greener grass, they also leech nutrients from the soil, expose it to harmful salts and acids, and create a weaker grass that is more susceptible to disease.

Toxic to family and pets

As you will see in the next chapter, healthy soil teems with microorganisms and insects that are essential to the production of grass that has strong blades and a vigorous root system. However, chemical pesticides kill the microorganisms needed to convert the nutrients found in fertilizers into the energy grass needs to grow. These toxic substances also kill the beneficial insects that play a role in pollination and consume the insects that can damage your lawn.

Another area of concern regarding the use of traditional lawn care products and methods is that some are downright dangerous to the health of humans and animals. They can cause a host of health problems, including eye and skin irritation, asthma and allergies, as well as an increased risk of diseases such as leukemia and other cancers. In fact, the active ingredient in most insecticides was originally developed for use in biological warfare.

Present in a large number of insecticides and herbicides is a group of chemical compounds known as organophosphates. Nazi and British nerve gas weapons used organophosphates. The active ingredient found in the deadly nerve gas is known as sarin.

The popularity of organophosphate insecticides grew after DDT, a pesticide that was the main competitor of organophosphate pesticides, was banned in the early 1970s. Organophosphate insecticides, which have not yet been banned, are now in widespread use today and are one of the leading causes of chemical poisoning. If you use on or more of the many insecticides and herbicides on the market today, your children, family members, and pets are being exposed to the equivalent of a small biological attack in your backyard.

Toxic to the environment

Not only are traditional lawn care methods dangerous to use around humans and animals, they also cause irreparable damage to the environment. Pesticide runoff from lawns often end up in nearby lakes, rivers, and streams, killing plant and fish species. Trees sprayed with pesticides harm birds and other wildlife that inhabit them. Prolonged use of pesticides results in pesticide buildup in the soil, which contaminates other species that were not the intended target of the pesticide. Over time, these pesticides move up the food chain as larger animals consume the smaller, contaminated ones and eventually wind up in our food supply.

Even chemical fertilizers can be toxic to the environment. Like pesticides, these fertilizers run off lawns when it rains or when watered and end up in nearby waterways. Once there, they promote the overgrowth of algae that uses up the water's available oxygen supply. The result? Native fish and plant species are oxygen starved and eventually die.

Expensive

And finally, the damage caused by using chemical fertilizers and pesticides, as well as harmful lawn maintenance techniques — for example, over-watering and mowing grass too short — makes grass more susceptible to disease and invasion by harmful insect species. As a result, homeowners who use these methods end up spending more money to treat these problems that would not exist if these chemicals were not used in the first place.

Benefits of Organic Lawn Care

Switching to organic lawn care methods and products is simply the smart thing to do. Homeowners have already seen the harm traditional lawn care methods cause. Here are some of the benefits organic lawn care can offer.

Healthy grass and soil

Organic lawn care is good for the soil. Organic-based nutrients are not fast acting like their synthetic counterparts; they are slowly released into the soil and provide the appropriate amount of food that grass needs to remain healthy and root systems require to grow strong and deep. Healthy soil teems with microorganisms beneficial to the soil, and these organisms help keep the soil from compacting, allow more oxygen supply to the roots, and increase root strength even more. The stronger the grass's root system becomes, the less opportunity there is for invasion by harmful bugs that can cause disease and other problems.

You have probably either seen or experienced the phenomenon known as "grass burn." This problem is caused by too much nitrogen in the soil, which causes the grass to wither and die. Organic lawn care eliminates this problem because any nitrogen contained in organic fertilizers is let out in the right amounts, so the grass is not overfed.

Safe for family and pets

Imagine having to tell your 3 year old she cannot play with Spot on the lawn today because you just applied an herbicide to get rid of that pesky crab grass. If you have a family and pets or simply enjoy entertaining friends and neighbors in your backyard, you do not want to have to limit these enjoyable, lawn-based activities because your lawn is soaked in chemical fertilizers and pesticides. Organic lawn care products eliminate the dangers associated with synthetic lawn care, which results in a healthy, beautiful, and safe outdoor haven your family and friends can enjoy year-round.

Safe for the environment

Organic lawn care products contain substances that are natural to the environment and, therefore, do not pose the serious toxic threat inherent in chemical fertilizers and pesticides. Because these substances are native to the environment, they will not harm anything when they biodegrade, which ensures the health of your lawn and the surrounding ecosystem. Fish, wildlife, and plant species, as well as people's food supplies, remain safe.

Low cost and low maintenance

Many people believe organic lawn care is more expensive than traditional lawn care, but nothing could be further from the truth. The National Wildlife Federation reports that 30 percent of the East Coast's water supply and 60 percent of the West Coast's water supply goes to watering lawns. That is the bad news. The good news is that organically cared for lawns require much less watering because the healthy soil retains moisture longer. The result is obvious: The less you need to water your lawn, the lower your water bill will be, and the more of this precious resource you will preserve for the generations to come.

Another cost benefit of organic lawn care is the fact that you will not need to mow your lawn as often as you do with traditional lawn care methods. Whether you own a gas-powered or electric lawn mower, you will either experience a lower electric bill or will not spend as much money on gasoline.

Because organic fertilizers are slow acting, you will not need to apply them as often. And, as you will soon see, organic lawn care amendments that improve the soil, such as compost, can be made at home from readily available ingredients, which further reduces the amount of money you spend buying products to feed your soil and grass.

Getting Started

Now that you understand why organic lawn care is a far superior choice than traditional lawn care methods, how can you get started? Not everyone can devote the time, attention, and money it takes to switch completely from traditional to organic lawn care. This book describes three options you can choose from, depending on your particular circumstances and your current lawn care situation.

The three options are:

1. Take a few steps to easy organic lawn care

2. Build an organic lawn from scratch

3. Transitioning a synthetic lawn to organic

Upcoming chapters will describe each of these approaches in detail, but here is a brief look at each one so you have an initial understanding of what to expect:

Option 1: Easy organic lawn care

With this option, you will simply take a few easy but critical steps to improve the health and safety of your lawn. Consider this approach if your lawn is in fairly decent condition but you want to withdraw it completely from chemical fertilizers and pesticides that might harm your family or pets. This option will not require a lot of your time, nor will you spend a lot of money to implement it.

You may also want to consider a special landscaping technique called xeriscaping you can apply to your lawn that is cost effective and requires little time to maintain. If you are short on time and money, this is the option for you. It is also an excellent option if you live in an area of the country where water is in short supply.

Option 2: Build an organic lawn from scratch

If time and expense are not issues, you might want to consider building an organic lawn from scratch. Choose this option especially if your lawn is in bad shape and nothing short of a complete overhaul will fix it. Your lawn may be toxic from years of chemical use, may be overgrown with weeds, or may not grow anything at all because the soil is in such poor condition.

You will need equipment and supplies over and above what the first two options required, so make sure your budget can handle all of the expenses you will accumulate. You will also need to be patient when using this approach because your lawn will not transform overnight. It may well take several years to complete the process, so you will need to be prepared to hang in there until it is finished.

Option 3: Transition a synthetic lawn to organic

Finally, you can choose to take a chemically dependant lawn and turn it into your organic masterpiece. Transitioning a synthetic lawn is an ambitious undertaking. You will need to purchase additional equipment and supplies and put a little more elbow grease into the process. This option is an excellent choice if your lawn is experiencing a few of the problems associated with traditional lawn care, such as grass burn or harmful insects and you want a safe way to address them. Choose this option if your lawn needs some work and you can invest the money it will take to accomplish it.

Before you explore each of these approaches, you will need to build your lawn on a solid foundation. The following chapters on soil, grass, and organic fertilizers will provide the information you need to create this critical base.

Chapter 2

HEALTHY SOIL

*I*n a natural environment, the soil underneath a lawn teems with life. In addition to all of the earthworms and other insects such as ants, beetles, and centipedes that are clearly visible when you dig a few inches into the earth, soil contains billions of microorganisms essential for the lawn's ability to nurture and support the grass and other plants on your lawn. Nematodes, bacteria, and algae are just a few of the microorganisms that flourish within healthy soil.

These microorganisms need food to survive, and the food these microscopic organisms eat comes from organic matter, either alive or dead. The complex interactions created when these microorganisms feed on the various insects and decayed plants, animals, and other microorganisms are known as the soil food web. Without these microorganisms, the soil will not have the ingredients it needs to grow healthy grass.

What is Soil Made of?

Soil consists of four ingredients: minerals from rocks in various states of decay, organic matter (e.g., decaying plant matter, worms, and microorganisms), water, and air. These components combine in varying degrees to create different soil types. The presence or absence of these components will also determine the relative health of your lawn's soil. *See Chapter 4 for information on how adding organic fertilizers to your soil will address mineral deficiencies.*

The top layer of soil on your lawn is called **topsoil**. Grass will send down roots into this topsoil in search of nutrients, water, and air. The level below topsoil is the denser subsoil, which does

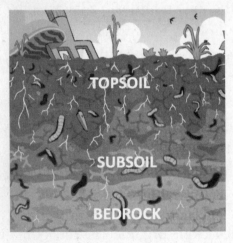

not have as many nutrients as topsoil and is much less porous, which prevents water from draining and air from circulating. Beneath subsoil is bedrock, the solid rock that makes up the earth's crust.

It is clear from these definitions that topsoil is where the action is. In addition to the correct proportion of nutrients, water, and air needed to promote healthy grass growth, your lawn's soil also needs to have the right texture and structure.

Texture

Texture refers to the amount of sand, silt, loam, and clay particles in soil.

- Sand consists of minerals and tiny pieces of rock created from erosion. Its constituent particles tend to be large, course, and gritty.

- Silt comes from quartz, and its particles are between the size of sand and clay particles. It often settles at the bottom of still bodies of water where it can mix with clay and organic matter. As a result, it is often extremely fertile.

- Clay also results from the decomposition of rock and the smallest mineral particles that, when wet, adhere together. People use it to make pots. When dry, it forms a hard substance that prevents water drainage and air circulation.

- Loam comes from equal parts of sand and silt with a little bit of clay added. It is the perfect medium for growing plants and grass; the sand creates enough space among the particles for air and water to circulate; the silt adds vital nutrients; and the clay helps hold the particles together to keep vital nutrients from washing away.

You can determine the texture of your soil by digging some up and handling it. How heavy or light does it feel? If it feels heavy and forms a solid mass when wet, it probably has a lot of clay content. If the particles are large, the soil feels light, and it filters easily through your fingers even when wet, you have sandy soil. Loamy soil has a weight between light sand and heavy clay; its particles will clump together when wet but break apart easily when handled.

Structure

Where soil texture refers to the size of the particles that make up the soil, structure refers to the extent to which soil particles adhere to each other. How well soil holds together depends in large part on how much organic matter it contains. Too little organic matter, and the nutrients in sandy soil wash away at the first rainfall. Clay becomes hard and compacted. And, the microorganisms that convert decaying matter into plant nutrients will be nonexistent because they do not have the food source they need for this important process.

Why is Healthy Soil Important?

When the microorganisms in the soil feed, they release carbon dioxide, nitrogen, and other byproducts of digestion that become the food your grass consumes. Therefore, you want to ensure these microorganisms continue to survive and thrive. The best way to keep these microorganisms well fed and happy is to give them an organic source of food.

There are four additional factors essential to your soil's health: depth, drainage, pH level, and nutrients.

Depth

The topsoil needs to be deep enough so the grass can develop a strong root system. Lawn soil found in the yards of most suburban homes consists of topsoil — the brown, crumbly dirt speckled with organic matter — and hard-packed sand and gravel, which is beneath the topsoil.

The best way to determine if your lawn has enough topsoil is to take a shovel and dig a hole. The topsoil will be some shade of brown, contain organic matter such as worms and decayed plants, and more or less crumble in your hands, but this will vary depending on the amount of sand, silt, and clay in your soil. Your lawn's grass needs 6 to 12 inches of topsoil to flourish. If your lawn does not contain enough topsoil, you can purchase topsoil from your local nursery or garden center, according the USDA. However, make sure the bag's label says it is free of weeds, insects, and disease. Sometimes housing and other developers will remove some of the topsoil from land being developed and sell it to nurseries that in turn sell it to the public. To be on the safe side, you can make your own topsoil by adding sand and sterilized manure to compost. *See Chapter 4 for more information on manure.*

Drainage

Good drainage is also essential to healthy soil. Drainage is created when the soil has a medium texture — as opposed to the heavy texture of clay or the light texture of sand — that allows water, nutrients, and air to move between the soil particles to get to the root system. You can improve poor drainage by adding gypsum, clay, compost, or sand to the soil.

PH level

The importance of the soil's pH level cannot be stressed enough. PH is an indicator of how acidic or alkaline the soil is, and it is measured on a scale of 0 to 14. Acidic soils have a pH between 0 and 7; alkaline soils are between 7 and 14. Depending on the part of the country you live in, your soil may be either excessively acid or alkaline. The ideal pH level for your lawn is between 6 and 7. The most accurate way to determine the pH level of your lawn's soil, as well as other nutrients your soil may need, is to test it.

Soil pH is important because soil is the medium through which nutrients are delivered to the grass, and these nutrients require a pH level around 6 or 7 to be most readily available to the grass.

Nutrients

Healthy soil contains two kinds of nutrients: macronutrients and micronutrients. **Macronutrients** are substances — such as nitrogen, phosphorous, potassium, calcium, sulfur, and magnesium — that plants need in large quantities to grow. **Micronutrients**, on the other hand, are substances plants need only in small quantities. These include iron, manganese, zinc, copper, molybdenum, boron, and chlorine. Soil needs macronutrients and micronutrients in the proper amounts to sustain healthy grass growth. *See Chapter 4 for information on what these nutrients are and which organic fertilizers are the best sources for them.*

Testing to Determine Soil Health

In addition to telling you the pH level of your lawn's soil, a soil test will also indicate the level of other nutrients your grass needs to grow properly. This information is extremely important because you will not know which organic products to purchase if you do not know in which nutrients your soil is deficient. You can certainly care for your lawn organically without getting the soil tested, as you will see in Chapter 5. However, if you plan to do more rehabilitation on your lawn than Chapter 5 calls for or you intend to start over from scratch, it makes sense to determine the current state of your soil before spending your hard-earned money on amendments your soil may need.

Types of soil tests

There are many kinds of soil tests available to homeowners. Below is a description of three different soil tests you can purchase from either your local Cooperative Extension Service or private lab. Each test provides specific information you may need, depending on your lawn care goals.

- **The standard soil test** will tell you the pH level of your soil and how much nitrogen, potassium, phosphorous, other nutrients, and organic matter the soil contains. Your state's Cooperative Extension Service will provide testing at a reasonable cost (around $10). Private laboratories may charge a little more (around $15).

  The test will also tell you which organic fertilizers to use, as well as the amounts to add to the soil to raise or lower the pH level and to provide the correct balance of nutrients. *You will learn more about these nutrients in greater detail in Chapter 4, the chapter on organic fertilizers.*

- The bioassay test is recommended for those who plan to overhaul the entire lawn. *This process is described in Chapter 7.* In addition to the information from the standard soil test, which provides pH and nutrient information, this test will tell you what kinds of microorganisms are in the soil and will advise you on how to correct any imbalances that might occur. This is an expensive test that costs $100 or more, but it will give you all of the information you need to determine the health and vitality of your lawn's soil.

- The soil life test is another inexpensive test that costs around $10. It will report on the level of microbial activity in your soil by measuring how much carbon dioxide is present. If microbial activity is low, you can add compost or compost tea to correct it.

The easiest way to find facilities in your area that will test your soil is to do an Internet search. Each state and territory is a part of the Department of Agriculture's Cooperative Extension System with offices in the state's land-grant university, as well as at the regional and local level. These offices provide educational information, as well as soil testing to agricultural producers, consumers, small businesses, and others.

To find the Cooperative Extension Service for your state, use the search terms, "Cooperative Extension" + (your state). Your state's Cooperative Extension Service can tell you the kinds of soil testing they perform and how much these tests cost. Some state institutions may even test your soil for free, so make sure to ask if free testing services are available.

The phone book is also a good source for locating private soil testing laboratories. If you have Internet access, simply type "soil testing," the city, and the state where you live in the search boxes at **www.yellowpages.com**. If you only have access to the hard copy directory, look under "soil testing" to find a private lab near you.

How to collect soil samples

The directions on your soil-test kit box will provide detailed instructions on collecting the soil sample and mailing it in for testing. For most soil tests, you will need a small shovel or spade for collecting the sample. Make sure any digging tool you use is free of rust and washed in distilled water before you collect the soil. If your collection tool is dirty or compromised by coming into contact with tap water or any liquid, the chemical composition of the soil could be dramatically altered.

The instructions will also advise you to collect soil in several spots around your lawn and dig 6 to 9 inches deep. Collect the

soil from different locations because its composition can vary from place to place. The best time to test your soil is when it is not too wet, too hot, or too cold. Ideally, collect your soil samples in the spring or fall.

These cores were drilled into the ground and then opened to test the soil samples.

If you decide to have your soil tested during other times of the year, collect the sample midmorning or late afternoon when the soil is neither too hot nor cold, and make sure the sample is moist but not soggy.

There is some disagreement on the amount of time that should elapse between when you gather the soil and send it in for testing. Some say to test the soil as quickly as possible, and others say the soil should be left out overnight. Still others say the soil should be frozen if it cannot be tested within a certain time. Just make sure to follow the instructions for collecting soil samples provided by the testing facility you have chosen to ensure the most accurate results possible.

Do-it-yourself or home soil-testing kits

The advantages to having a laboratory test your soil is these facilities can test for all of the various macronutrients and micronutrients present in your lawn. Most home testing kits will only test for pH levels and/or the basic nitrogen-phosphorous-potassium nutrient trio present in most fertilizers. However, depending on the level and intensity of lawn care you intend to undertake, you may need more information about the soil's nutrient levels and microbial activity than these kits can provide. Why not spend the $10 or so on a test that will give you far more reliable information and that requires less labor on your part?

On the other hand, if you are a do-it-yourself kind of person, you can find these tests at most nurseries and garden centers. Make sure you follow the instructions as carefully as you can to get the most accurate results possible.

Compost

Compost is one of the best ingredients you can add to your soil. It ensures the soil contains the vital mix of nutrients it needs to keep your grass strong and healthy. Compost also provides the soil texture and structure that promotes proper depth and good drainage. Many people believe compost is an organic fertilizer. In fact, it is a **soil amendment**, something added to the soil to boost its organic content. Remember that all of the microorganisms in the soil need a food source they convert into the macro and micronutrients the plants feed on. Compost supplies this food source in a decomposed state.

Benefits of using compost

The benefits and advantages of using compost are vital. Compost:

- Releases nutrients at a much slower rate than synthetic fertilizers and promotes sustained plant growth over a long time

- Optimizes the soil's pH level by neutralizing soils that are either too acidic or too alkaline

- Improves the texture and structure of soil so air, water, and nutrients are easily transported throughout the soil

- Prevents soil erosion by encouraging healthy root systems

- Provides a rich source of nutrients, such as nitrogen, when bacteria break down organic matter and convert it into food

- Improves the health of the soil, making grass less susceptible to disease and pests

- Provides an excellent means of recycling the dead branches, leaves, lawn, shrubbery clippings, and other cuttings that result from regular lawn maintenance

Compost also adds vital humus to the topsoil. **Humus** is the organic matter in compost that has finished decaying. It is where 99 percent of all grass growth occurs.

It certainly makes sense to add compost to your lawn because the money you spend either buying or making it is offset by the fact that you will not need to spend nearly as much money on pesticides to get rid of the damaging weeds, insects, and disease that proliferate in unhealthy or lifeless soil.

Commercially available compost

The two main types of compost available for use on your lawn are the ones you purchase and the ones you make. Commercially available compost is sold in 40-pound bags and can be purchased at your local nursery or garden center. This commercially available compost will vary in terms of quality and price. Do not automatically assume you will save money by purchasing the cheapest compost you can find. You want compost rich in organic matter, and that may mean spending a little more than you might want to.

How do you know which brand of compost is the best one to buy? Apply this four-question test to the compost you are considering to help you decide.

- **How does it feel?** You want compost to have a loose texture that will sift through your fingers like grains of sand. Any wood and bark used to make it should be completely decomposed. You want the compost to be loose enough to spread easily on your lawn.

- **What color is it?** Look for compost that has a rich, dark-brown color. Dark color is important because the darker the compost, the more organic matter it contains.

- **How wet is it?** Make sure the compost your purchase is moist but not soggy or dry. Soggy, overly wet compost is difficult to spread, and if the compost is too wet, you will end up buying more water than organic material. If the compost appears heavily clumped in the bag, it probably has too much water in it, and you do not want to buy it.

- **How does it smell?** How the compost smells is an indication of its maturity. You want compost that smells as earthy and rich as possible. If the compost emits a strong, unpleasant odor, this indicates that the organic material has not decayed and will not be good for your grass. Your compost should not be hot and steamy, as this is another indication of compost that has not fully matured.

Some of these questions will be difficult to answer because the manufacturer bags the compost. Consider asking your garden center if there is any unbagged compost you can inspect. If this is not possible, ask the store what its refund policy is if you discover the compost does not live up to the quality the packaging or the store's advertisements imply. On the other hand, if you find the compost has not matured sufficiently when you get it home and the store will not provide a refund on an opened bag, add it to your backyard compost pile if you have one, and allow it to ripen.

Another option is to buy the compost in bulk quantities, especially if you have a large area to cover. Not only will it save you multiple trips to the garden center, but you will also be able to inspect the compost before delivery to ensure it is of the highest quality. Check your local garden center to ascertain if bulk compost is available for purchase, and if not, where it is available.

Another concern when purchasing compost is to avoid compost that contains animal products, such as manure. If your compost contains this material, handle it with gloves and protective outerwear. Wash your hands and any protective clothing thoroughly once you have finished applying it.

An excellent way to ensure the compost you purchase contains no pesticides is to look for the Organic Materials Review Institute (OMRI) seal on the package. OMRI is a nonprofit group that reviews agricultural products to ensure those claiming to be organic abide by the rules the National Organic Program (NOP) established. The NOP, created by the Department of Agriculture and the National Organic Standards Board, forbids the use of artificial fertilizers and pesticides in products that claim to be organic.

Do-It-Yourself Compost

You also have the option of creating your own compost from scratch. When it comes to creating and maintaining the natural balance of the ecosystem around your home, there is no better option available. Instead of leaving grass clippings and other refuse resulting from lawn maintenance for the trash collector, deposit them in a compost pile or bin and create an inexpensive food source for your lawn.

Creating a compost pile can be a rewarding experience the entire family can participate in. Little Tonya can collect small branches and twigs for this week's new compost batch while Curtis rakes some of the dead leaves from the front yard. It can also serve as an excellent educational activity for children. Composting will teach them all about the life cycle of the plants, insects, and other components that make up the compost pile.

Where to store composting material

To begin composting at home, the first thing you need is a receptacle for the decaying, organic matter that will one day become compost for your lawn. The choice of where to do your composting on your property will be determined in part by where you live. If you live in a deed-restricted suburb, your neighbors are probably not going to appreciate that pile of rotting materials in your backyard. On the other hand, residents of a more rural setting may think nothing of it.

Situate your pile in an area of your property that is not too shady or closed in and where it will not get too wet. If your area gets a lot of rain, try to place it under a structure to keep it relatively dry and still permit air circulation. A damp, dark, enclosed space is the perfect breeding ground for the bacteria that will have your compost pile stinking in no time. You will also want to place it in an area where it will not attract too much attention and have the neighbors complaining.

After you decide where to place your compost pile, you will need to decide if your compost pile is going to be free standing, out in the open, or contained in a bin.

Free-standing pile

Free-standing compost piles do not have to be messy. If you choose to go this route, you can always enclose it in wire fencing to keep its contents from spilling out. The size of the pile will depend, in part, on the size of your lawn and how much organic matter it generates for your compost pile because a lot of this organic material will be grass clippings. It will also depend on how many trees and shrubs are on your property; the more your yard has, the more branches, bark, leaves, and twigs you will be able to add to the compost pile. Keep in mind that as decomposition occurs, the pile will shrink in size, so do not be discouraged if it takes a while to build up enough compost to cover your lawn.

You also want to ensure proper water drainage in a free-standing pile. One way to accomplish this is to dig a hole as wide as the base your compost pile will be and several inches deep. Cover this area with sturdy wire mesh. Then, add your compost material on top of it. You will still have to turn the pile frequently so that wet material at the bottom and center of the pile gets moved up and toward the exterior of the pile where it can receive enough air to prevent too much water accumulation.

Compost bins

 The other option is to purchase a compost bin. Not only does a bin keep the compost out of sight and protected from rainfall, but many bins also include a mechanism that lets you spin or tumble the decaying matter to keep it well aerated. *You will learn more about turning the compost later in this chapter.* The bin is attached to hinges that, in turn, are mounted on legs or some other support on either side of the bin. A handle is attached to one of the hinges, and this handle lets you turn the bin and tumble the organic matter inside.

Check your local nursery, garden center, or discount store for composter bins they offer. You can purchase an 80-gallon bin at some retailers for as little as $50. Of course, the larger the bin's capacity, the more expensive it will be. The website GREENCulture™ (**www.composters.com**) is another source of excellent information on composter bins and supplies.

Something as simple as a trash bin can serve as a compost bin. The lid will protect the compost from rainfall, but you will need to punch holes in the sides to make sure the compost gets enough air. If you opt not to punch holes in the side, keep the lid off the trash can and replace it when you aerate the compost. To do this, simply shake the contents by hand after some decomposition has occurred.

Finally, you can construct a compost bin from wooden pallets. At a minimum, you will need three pallets and some wire. To make a compost bin from pallets, place the pallets on their edges so the three resemble a giant cube with no top and one side missing. If you use four pallets, simply place them on their edges so they resemble a giant cube with only the top missing. Secure the pallets where their edges meet with some wire.

What to include in your compost pile

You can include a variety of organic material in your compost pile. This includes "green" matter such as grass clippings and weeds rich in nitrogen, as well as "brown" matter consisting of dead leaves, bark, and twigs that provide carbon. Just make sure you have more brown matter than green, preferably in a 2:1 ratio. Keeping your organic matter in this proportion will keep the pile from smelling. You can also include:

- Seaweed

- Sawdust

- Animal manure

- Weeds

- Hay and straw

- Coffee grounds

- Newspaper and other untreated paper products

Break up large pieces of organic material — branches, tree bark — into smaller pieces. This will increase the speed at which it decomposes. If you include garbage from your kitchen table, be sure to remove any meat, dairy, or oily foods because these will not only attract critters you do not want roaming across your lawn, but it will stink as well. Include some soil from your yard because it will contain microorganisms native to the area that will more easily adapt to the compost pile. You might also consider adding some organic fertilizer rich in nitrogen or compost tea, which will be discussed later, to accelerate decomposition.

How to maintain your compost pile

Turning and tumbling

Do not expect compost to happen overnight. It takes time and patience, but if properly aerated, the process will go much more quickly than a pile that has not received enough air, often in as little as a month's time. This is because the organisms that break down the organic material in your compost pile need air to breathe. The more air they have, the more rapid the decay of organic material, and the less the compost pile will smell. Aeration also keeps the compost pile from becoming too soggy.

You can use a pitch fork to turn the composting material.

To aerate your compost properly, you will need to turn it (in free-standing piles or cans) or tumble it (in a tumbler bin) to ensure maximum aeration.

- If you have a free-standing compost pile, use a rake to stir up the compost, employing either the rake end or the handle end. As the compost approaches maturity, a shovel or spade might work better because the compost will be close to the consistency of soil. If you are not afraid to get your hands dirty, put on an old, long-sleeve shirt and some sturdy gloves and mix the compost by hand.

- If the compost is in a bin or other container, you will need to turn the organic matter with a rake or shovel so material at the bottom and center of the bin gets redistributed toward the outside and top.

- If you are using a tumbler bin, simply turn the handle or the bin to tumble the compost.

When a free-standing compost pile is small, about 3 feet high by 3 feet wide by 3 feet long, you will probably want to turn or tumble it every three to five days. As the pile becomes larger, you will aerate it less and less because there will be simply too much organic matter to make this feasible. Do not let this concern you; the maturing compost will contain a wealth of worms and insects crawling through it to aerate it for you. Just remember, the more you turn the compost, the more air it gets, allowing it to decompose more quickly.

Whether in a bin or free-standing pile, if your compost pile begins to emit a foul odor, you will need to turn or tumble it every day until the smell goes away. Adding more brown material to the bin will also improve the smell, but rotation is key to keeping the matter decomposing.

Moisture

You will need to closely monitor the amount of water your compost pile contains. When the compost is too wet, water replaces air, depriving microorganisms of the air they need to breathe. On the other hand, too little water deprives them of the water they need to break down organic matter. Therefore, the compost should be kept moist, with a 40 to 60 percent water content. A handful of compost should feel like a damp sponge, but you should not be able to squeeze water out of it.

Heat

The decomposition of organic matter in a compost pile produces heat. The temperature of the pile needs to be high enough, somewhere between 131 and 150 degrees, to destroy weed seeds and plant pathogens, organisms that cause disease in plants. You can purchase a thermometer to keep track of the pile's temperature at your local nursery, garden center, or online for as little as $15.

If your compost pile has one of the following characteristics, it should reach temperatures high enough to ensure quick decomposition of the organic matter within the compost pile:

- Has the right mix of carbon- and nitrogen-producing organic matter — in a 2:1 ratio

- Is the right size — at least 3 feet by 3 feet by 3 feet

- Has enough but not too much water

- Is sufficiently aerated

PH level

It is a good idea to test the pH level of the compost from time to time during the decomposition process to help ensure the compost has the proper pH level that will benefit your lawn. You can determine its pH level either by sending a sample to your local lab or conducting a pH test yourself.

If you decide to do the test yourself, you can purchase pH strips from your local nursery or garden center. The test is fairly simple to administer. Place a strip into the moist compost, wait a few seconds, and then remove it. The strip will turn a specific color that you then match to the chart of pH color levels that came with the strips. If you have added the right ingredients in the right amounts, the pH level of your compost should be between 6 and 7. However, if the compost is too acidic, toward the 0 end of the pH scale, you can add lime to the mix to correct it; if it is too alkaline, toward the 14 end of the scale, add sulfur.

When to apply compost

If the grass on your lawn looks healthy and has few brown spots, you probably do not need to add compost. However, soil testing, in addition to the overall condition of your grass, will help you make an informed decision about whether you need to apply it.

Lawn care experts agree lawns should have a fresh layer of compost applied two to three times a year, normally in the fall before the first big freeze and in the spring to support plant growth. However, depending on grass type, climate, and the intensity of the seasons, the times and frequency of compost application could vary widely. The Environmental Protection Agency (EPA) has provided specific regional information on when to apply compost by state at its website, **www.epa.gov**. At this site, individuals will learn the types of compost materials and methods that are acceptable and encouraged within each state.

How to apply compost once it is "done"

When your compost has finished decomposing, it should have the consistency of a moist, dark, finely textured soil. If the compost is too lumpy, it will sit on top of the grass and not get down into the soil. It should crumble into tiny bits of manageable debris when handled. The compost needs to be able to fall easily between the blades of grass and onto the ground where it can readily mix with the topsoil.

How much will you need?

Before applying the compost, you will need to determine how much you will need. Commercial compost is sold in 40-pound bags, but the amount of compost you need is measured in cubic feet. A 40-pound bag of moist — not too wet or dry — compost is about 1 cubic foot, but check the bag label to determine how many cubic feet of compost it contains. With this information, you can calculate how many cubic feet of compost you will need to cover your lawn:

- Calculate the area of your lawn in square feet: length of yard x width of yard = square footage.

- Decide how thick you want to apply the compost — ½ to 1 inch for new lawns; ¼ to ½ inch on existing lawns.

- Convert the thickness into feet by dividing the thickness by 12 — e.g., ½ inch divided by 12 = .04 feet; 1 inch divided by 12 = .08 feet.

- Multiply this thickness by the area — in square feet — you want to cover. This will give you a measure of your lawn in cubic feet.

For example, you have a lawn that is 20 feet wide and 20 feet long, which equals 400 square feet. You decide to apply compost ½ inch (.04 feet) thick: 400 multiplied by .04 equals 16 cubic feet, which means you will need about 16 bags of commercial compost to cover your lawn. Purchasing this amount of commercial compost can be expensive, not to mention extremely heavy to load into your car. You will cut down on cost by either making it or buying it in bulk or using a combination of commercial, bulk, and homemade.

How to apply your compost

The following instructions describe how to apply compost on an existing lawn.

1. Apply the compost over the entire lawn area. You will probably need a wheelbarrow and shovel or rototiller to do this. If too much of the compost is in one area, redistribute it to parts of the lawn that need more compost or put it back in the compost pile or bin for later use.

2. After distributing the compost, smooth it out with a leaf rake. Do this delicately so the blades of grass and the underlying root structure remain intact and not damaged.

3. After raking, water the lawn lightly. You do not need to soak the lawn after applying compost, something that synthetic fertilizers require. The nutrients in the compost release slowly, and you do not want to flush them away with too much water.

4. Do not mow the lawn for at least a week to give the compost time to settle down between the grass blades.

You will learn more about how to apply compost in Chapters 6 and 7, which describe the work involved in rehabilitating your lawn and building an organic lawn from scratch.

Compost Tea

Another option for feeding your lawn is to make **compost tea**, which is a liquid version of compost. Compost tea is a powerful addition to your organic lawn care program because it contains plant nutrients suspended in the liquid and, therefore, more immediately available to your grass than they are in dry compost. Compost tea is also teeming with beneficial microorganisms that get sprayed into the soil and onto the grass blades, which allows them to begin digesting organic matter and converting it into more nutrients. Finally, compost tea serves as an **inoculant**, which means it helps prevent the growth and spread of disease.

You can buy the tea at your local nursery or gardening center or make it at home. When you consider the ingredients you will need to create the tea and the low cost associated with making this product, it makes sense to make a compost tea brewer and then make your own tea. Purchasing the tea can be expensive, and some stores charge more than $30 for one container of compost concentrate.

Although there are numerous brands of compost tea brewers for sale on the Internet, they are all fairly expensive so only consider buying one if you have the extra money to spend. *See the Appendix, which includes several websites that offer compost tea brewers for sale.* The average price can range from $100 to $500. On the other hand, compost tea brewers are easy to make, and you can make one with supplies that you already have at home.

How to make compost tea

Follow these easy steps to make compost tea.

1. Get a 5-gallon plastic bucket or drum, and fill it with water.

2. Get a mesh bag or a pair of stockings, fill it with high-quality compost, and put it in the water. The bag or stocking only needs to be about 3 to 5 inches wide and

approximately 12 to 16 inches long. Over time and through trial and error, you will be able to determine the correct amount of compost to use to make your tea. You can adjust the amount of compost to alter the quality, richness, and density of your tea.

3. Find an old fish tank aerator. Before buying one, ask your family and neighbors to see if they have one that they would be willing to give you. If you do not have an aerator and cannot find someone to give you one, you can buy one from almost any pet or variety store for around $10.

4. Insert the aerator's hose into the 5-gallon drum so it will pump oxygen into the water. Place the aerator in an area where it will not be accidentally knocked into the water, such as on a shelf or mounted to a wall. Also, place the drum far enough away from the aerator so if the water in the drum spills, it will not touch the aerator or its power cord. It is a good idea to purchase a long hose to run from your aerator so the aerator can be positioned a safe distance away from the water-filled bucket.

5. Plug the aerator in, and turn it on.

The tea will take two to three days to brew with the aerator running constantly. Good compost tea smells sweet and earthy.

If your tea starts to smell bad, there is not enough oxygen circulating in the water, which creates too much ammonia in the compost. Try turning the aerator pump to a higher setting. If this does not work, add another aerator to the water, and stir it frequently until the smell goes away. Never use bad-smelling compost tea on your lawn. If you cannot get rid of the smell, start a new batch, and make sure it is well aerated.

How to apply compost tea to your lawn

When the tea is ready, remove the bag and hose from the liquid, and pour the tea into empty spray bottles you have sanitized beforehand. Then, let your children have their own "compost tea spraying party." However, make sure the children spray the lawn and not each other.

If you do not have empty spray bottles at home, you can purchase them just about anywhere — at your grocery story, big box discount store, or garden center. You can also use a siphon attached to a garden hose to distribute the compost tea on your lawn. Finally, you can use the sprinklers that water your lawn to apply the tea. With these last two methods, the tea is being filtered through water, so you may want to prepare an extra strong batch so the water does not dilute its strength.

Vermicomposting

Vermicomposting is a method of creating compost that uses worms to consume food waste and other organic material that it then eliminates in the form of "castings." You can apply these nutrient-rich castings to your lawn in the same way you would apply commercial or homemade compost. You can also mix it with compost from your compost bin or with store-bought compost to enrich its quality and nutrient content.

This form of composting produces the most biologically active compost available and is the cream of the compost crop. And, believe it or not, it is fairly easy to make, though you can purchase it at your local nursery, garden center, farming supply store, or bait store.

Homemade vermicompost

If you have the time, a climate-controlled storage space, and the will to pursue such a project, homemade vermicompost would be a healthy part of an organic lawn care system. If you do not have a climate-controlled area in which to store your worms but still want to use vermicompost, your best option is to purchase the compost from a local retailer. Always keep in mind the worms you will use are living creatures that need food, care, attention, and the proper environment in which to survive. If you decide to create vermiform compost at home, remember that you are essentially adopting hundreds of tiny new pets that need the care and respect you would give to your dog or cat.

Instructions for making vermicompost at home

The first thing you will need to get started are worm bins you can purchase online from sites such as Uncle Jim's Worm Farm (**http://unclejimswormfarm.com**) and WormsWrangler (**http:// wormswrangler.com**). It is more time consuming and difficult to find a local retailer for worm bins because of the limited number of retailers; however, most of the bins found online are more expensive than bins sold at a hardware store. The great thing about these worm bins is they include holes already drilled into them that allow the worms to breathe.

You can also create worm bins by using large plastic storage bins — around 3 feet by 2 feet by 1 foot — that also have a lid. These are available at a wide range of stores, as well as online. Purchase three or more, and place them in a dark, cool spot in your garage or shed. You will need to drill holes in the sides of the bin near the top and lid so the worms have air to breathe. Although you could use cardboard boxes and place garbage bags inside them, this type of composting structure could easily leak or become extremely flimsy and is not recommended for vermicomposting.

Temperature and location

Ideally, the temperature where you store your worm bins should be between 50 to 80 degrees, which is why a garage or shed provides an ideal location. The location should have some type of climate control to make sure the worms do not get too hot or cold. You could place the worms inside the house; however, it is a better idea to keep them in a location where you do not have to worry about them escaping.

Bedding

After you have the worm bins and the right location, you will need to make your worms' bedding. Newspaper is ideal for this. Shred enough paper to fill half the bin, but make sure you do not cover up the ventilation holes at the top of the bin. Next, you will need to add water. The basic formula is two parts water to one part paper. The paper should be moist but not so wet that it drips. If you think your paper is too dry, you can always add more water. Make sure to use only newspaper and not glossy magazine paper the worms can get stuck to. You will also need to add a gritty substance, such as soil and sand, that the worms will use to grind their food because they have no teeth.

Which worms to buy

After you have prepared your bins, the next thing you will need to do is find your worms. You can purchase them from a bait store, buy them from garden centers and nurseries, or order them online. The websites mentioned before that sell worm bins also offer Red Wigglers for sale. Do not use the earthworms found in your yard. These are called "night crawlers" and eat slower than Red Wigglers. Night crawlers need cooler temperatures. These worms also need an extensive tunneling system to survive and cannot survive in a worm bin. To speed up decomposition, you can add about 1 cup of soil rich in microorganisms. When you are ready to add the worms to the bin, make sure to place them about one-third to two-thirds of the way down into the material, cover them up, and let them adapt to their new home.

Feeding the worms

Feeding Red Wigglers and harvesting their castings makes a fun project for children. Feed the worms fruit and vegetable scraps, as well as coffee and tea grounds, once every week. Avoid adding animal and dairy products because these can cause the bin to smell. You want to add food scraps in the right amount so the worms have enough to eat but not too much. If they cannot consume all of the food you give them, it will start to rot and cause your bin to smell. A good rule of thumb is to feed them ½ pound of food scraps for every pound of worms in your bin.

Harvesting castings

To harvest the castings, gently move the newspaper bedding to one side just before the weekly feeding. Place a new batch of food into the now empty potion of the bin. Wait a week or two for all of the worms to move to where the new food is, and then remove the castings from the side of the bin they traveled from. You might want to wear gloves for this process, but it is not necessary. Examine the freshly harvested castings, and make sure there are no worms in them. Also, by positioning a light on the bin, the worms will naturally burrow to the bottom away from the light source. If there are worms in the harvestings, remove them, and place them back into the bin. After you harvest the castings, add fresh newspaper strips, water, and soil into the bin, and let the circle of life continue.

Now that you have a good idea what the right mixture of soil is, the next step in the process is to learn about grass itself. With the soil balanced, the grass is the next logical step in transforming your yard.

CASE STUDY:
LIZ JOHNSTON

Liz Johnston, The Greener Good
Contact: Andrea Morin
Hutson Creative
817-470-0922
andrea@hutsoncreative.com

The Greener Good provides resources on how to live a green life, including educational products and services to help individuals be healthier. An expert in the field of organic lawn care, Liz Johnston from The Greener Good offered an interesting opinion on the reason organic lawn care is so beneficial.

Johnston said, "Our current ambivalence to what we are putting into the ground and ultimately our bodies through chemical pesticides and fertilizers seems to coordinate with our ambivalence to what we are throwing in the trash. It's a funny relationship between our trash and the health of our food supply and yards. If we are conscious of what we are throwing away and what we are recycling into our lawns and gardens, we could completely negate the need for the harmful chemicals added to the commercially available food supply. I am talking about compost. It is such an easy and cost-effective idea."

One of the areas she focuses on teaching people about is care for the earth through recycling. This is important in terms of composting but also in daily life. She says, "Daily trash in the United States has doubled over the past 40 years. The average person in this country is throwing out 4.5 pounds of trash per day. That adds up to more than 250 million tons of trash per year. What is even more shocking than that colossal number is that more than 12.7 percent of that trash is from food waste. An additional 13.2 percent is from yard trimmings. That is a quarter of the annual trash deposited in our landfills or roughly 62.5 million tons of trash. That is such a huge number that it seems immeasurable, but to put it into perspective, it is equivalent to 62.5 million Volkswagen Beetles, 9 million elephants, or 284 baseball stadiums!"

We can take a bite out of that huge amount of waste by focusing on composting, as discussed throughout this book. It starts in the home, as Johnston states but carries through to the earth as well.

"Composting requires a commitment to be conscious of what you are eating and what you are throwing away. All of your produce scraps, egg shells, coffee grounds, and even paper can be composted in your own backyard. What's even more exciting is you can create wildly beneficial compost in a very short amount of time. By responsibly composting our kitchen scraps and yard trimmings, we can keep all that excess trash out of the landfills."

As you take into consideration the value of composting, consider what it can offer to the soil itself. Johnston says composting is one of the essential steps to ensuring a healthy garden. She explains, "Unlike synthetic fertilizers, compost contains both macro and micronutrients and releases these nutrients slowly over months or even years. Compost also neutralizes both acidic and alkaline soils and provides beneficial soil structure. It also brings and feeds diverse life in the soil, such as bacteria, fungi, insects, worms, and more that support healthy plant growth."

Sometimes, looking at the way a person lives his or her life is the best way understand a person's message. Johnston's skills in educating others about the benefits of living a healthy life come through in her work and are important to the organic lawn care sector. She said, "As an advocate for greener trends in all aspects of life, I define organic lawn care as any effort put forth to reduce our water pollution and soil corruption and any effort to improve the health and safety of our families and lawn care workers. To me, organic gardening isn't daunting; it is practical and can save you a lot of money. Organic lawn care and gardening not only reduces the chemical exposure brought on by the use of synthetic fertilizers and pesticides, but it also costs less and benefits our planet for the long haul."

Chapter 3

THE RIGHT GRASS

The second ingredient that forms the foundation of your organic lawn care program is grass. But not just any grass. It is important to select the right grass for your lawn. Many factors affect which variety of grass will be the best choice, including:

- The climate of the region in which you live

- The availability of water in your geographical area

- The type of soil in your part of the country

- The use(s) to which you will put your lawn

- Your expectations about how you want your lawn to look

These factors boil down to two primary considerations: the region of the country in which you live and how you intend to use your lawn. As for the last factor in the above list, though you want your lawn to look as beautiful as possible, you may have to lower your expectations a bit. Organic lawn care will produce strong, healthy grass, but do not expect your lawn to look like a putting green. That bright green carpet might be what traditional lawn care has conditioned us to think grass is supposed to look like; however, as you read in Chapter 1, this perfect-looking lawn is in fact the result of poor nutrition and unhealthy lawn care practices.

Types of Grass

There are many ways to break up the United States into regions to classify the different types of grass. One method divides the country into five distinct regions: the Northeast; the South, including Hawaii; the Great Plains; the Southwest; and the Northwest, including Alaska. Another, simpler method used in this book is to base the classification on climate. This classification system results in three basic grass types:

- Cool season grasses are best suited for the upper half of the continental United States and Alaska, where the climate tends to be on the cold side. These grasses do best when the temperature is between 50 and 80 degrees. Temperatures that are hotter or colder than this range will most likely turn grass brown, especially in the absence of adequate rainfall.

- Warm season grasses grow well in the southern-most quarter of the United States and Hawaii, where the climate is warm to hot. These grasses thrive in hot temperatures, as long as water is available. Otherwise, they will turn brown during periods of drought.

- Transitional grasses work best in the remaining quarter of the United States, in the middle of the cold and warm regions where the climate is moderate but can also vary widely depending on factors such as rainfall and elevation.

The table below indicates which states fall into these three areas.

These grass types ...	Work best in these states ...
Cool Season	Alaska; upper two-thirds of California; the lower quarter of Nevada; Utah; the upper three-quarters of Colorado; the upper quarter of Missouri; the upper two-thirds of Illinois, Indiana, and Ohio; Pennsylvania; New Jersey; and all of the states north of these.
Warm Season	Hawaii; the lower quarter of Arizona and New Mexico; the lower two-thirds of Texas; Louisiana; Mississippi; Alabama; Georgia; South Carolina; and Florida.
Transitional	Lower third of California; the upper three-quarters of Nevada; the lower quarter of Colorado; the upper three-quarters of Arizona and New Mexico; the upper third of Texas; Oklahoma; Kansas; the lower three-quarters of Missouri; the lower third of Illinois, Indiana, and Ohio; Kentucky; Tennessee; North Carolina; Virginia; West Virginia; Maryland; Delaware; and Washington D.C.

The above table is a rough approximation of the geographical areas best suited to these three grass types. If you are not sure which grass(es) will work best on your lawn, check with your local Cooperative Extension Service, nursery, or garden center before making a selection.

The following grasses represent the main varieties included in these three categories.

Cool season grasses

For best results, different types of cool season grasses are blended together to build up their resistance to pests, drought, cold weather, weeds, and disease. It is rare for an application of cool season grasses to be of only one variety.

Kentucky bluegrass

Although the slender blades of Kentucky bluegrass produce a lush, beautiful, dark-green lawn, its root system does not grow as deeply as other grasses and, as a result, needs a lot more watering and fertilizing. Because it does not hold nutrients and water well, it is often mixed with ryegrass and fescues in order to create a stronger, more durable lawn. Many varieties or cultivars of Kentucky bluegrass are bred for specific qualities, such as drought and shade tolerance, turf thickness, and so on. If you are determined to have a Kentucky bluegrass lawn, your local nursery or garden center can help you make a selection that best meets the needs of the climate, soil, and conditions in your area.

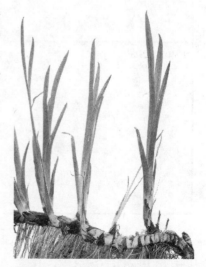

Example of a rhizome stem from grass

Kentucky bluegrass can grow 18 to 24 inches tall and spreads by rhizomes, forming a dense sod. Root growth begins when temperatures are about 60 degrees, and growth will cease once temperatures are at 80 degrees. There are more than 100 varieties of Kentucky bluegrass available, and blending several varieties of grass is better than using only one variety because all the variations of this grass are not all affected by harmful conditions at once. Plant 2 to 3 pounds of seeds per 1,000 square feet of lawn area you would like to cover. Although you can plant this grass year-round, it is best to plant in the spring and fall.

Perennial ryegrass

Dark-green and thick, perennial ryegrass sprouts fairly quickly and will grow faster than weeds, thus keeping them out of your lawn. It can also wear well, taking a lot of foot traffic, but needs sunlight, good drainage, and acidic soil to thrive. When purchasing perennial ryegrass, make sure you do not confuse it with annual ryegrass that grows quickly but will die during prolonged periods of cold or heat. Check the label of any grass product you purchase to ensure you selected the correct variety. They will tolerate periods of low moisture and high temperatures but will not do well in areas that have extended periods of temperatures higher than 90 degrees.

Fescues

Highly versatile, drought- and often shade-tolerant, fescues come in several varieties, each with distinct characteristics.

Turf-type, tall fescue, not to be confused with its pasture-grass predecessor, holds its dark green color during most of the year. A low-maintenance grass that does not require a lot of nitrogen, it can be brought back after a hot summer by adding more seed to an existing lawn (called **overseeding**) or will recover on its own when the weather warms up after a cold spell. It can develop a deep root system that allows it to tolerate periods of drought easily. Unlike non-turf-forming fescues that tend to clump, this fescue creates a smooth, even lawn that can take its share of foot traffic.

Creeping red fescue, also dark green in color and often mixed with tall-fescue and blues, makes a good lawn grass because of its ability to spread or creep across the lawn and eliminate gaps in coverage. It does not tolerate heat or foot traffic as well as turf-type tall fescue, but it does not require as much sunlight. It is also low maintenance and tolerates drought conditions well, and you can use it exclusively to create a fine-looking lawn.

The most shade tolerant of the fescues is chewings fescue. Unlike creeping red and turf-type tall fescue, it grows in clumps and cannot bear much foot traffic. The more sun it has, the easier it can spread across the lawn. It is also low maintenance and fairly drought tolerant.

Finally, hard fescue, as the name implies, is cold and heat tolerant. Hard fescue grass grows slowly and in clumps, is blue-green in color, is highly disease resistant, and is shade and drought tolerant.

Warm season grasses

Unlike their cool season counterparts, manufacturers do not mix warm season grasses together. Applying only one grass seed is common because they differ widely in rate of growth, color, and appearance. The two most widely used warm season grasses are Bermuda and St. Augustine.

Bermuda grass

This is the grass most often found on Southern golf course fairways. A fast-growing grass, it needs lots of sunlight to thrive and will take a high degree of foot traffic, which makes it an excellent grass for families with children. It is, however, a high-maintenance grass that requires a lot of mowing and nitrogen to keep it green. The soil needs to be rich in organic matter and microbial activity, which will produce the nitrogen it needs naturally instead of resorting to synthetic fertilizers.

Bermuda grass grows best in areas where average daily temperatures are about 75 degrees. The optimal daytime temperature for this type of grass is 95 to 100 degrees. For the plant to begin growing properly, soil temperatures need to be a minimum of 65 degrees, but 80 degrees is best for plant growth. It grows best in areas with between 25 and 100 inches of rainfall each year and in areas where the average rainfall is less than 20 inches; irrigations methods are required to allow the grass to grow properly. Bermuda grass can grow in a myriad of soil conditions, including deep sands and heavy soils, as long as the soils are fertile.

St. Augustine grass

A high-maintenance grass that requires frequent fertilizing and mowing, St. Augustine grass can only be planted as sod because the seeds are not commercially available. This grass grows fast and spreads quickly, tolerates moderate shade, and handles a moderate amount of foot traffic. On the other hand, it does not resist weeds or insects well. Because it requires so much mowing, fertilizing, and pest control — all great money-makers for commercial landscapers steeped in traditional lawn care methods — it is not the best grass for an organic lawn.

St. Augustine grows best in moist, coastal areas with mild winter temperatures and tolerates high summer temperatures. It can grow in soil with pH levels ranging from 5.0 to 8.5 but does not tolerate compacted or overly saturated conditions. It will need supplemental irrigation in areas of the country that receive less than 30 inches of rainfall each year.

Bahia grass

An excellent grass for an organic lawn, Bahia grass is not only drought resistant but also disease and pest resistant. It needs little fertilizer, grows in a wide range of soil types, requires little mowing, and tolerates foot traffic well. Although it may not produce as attractive a blade as St. Augustine, its low maintenance characteristics make it a far superior choice for the homeowner interested in promoting environmentally friendly lawn care practices. It is commonly identified by its Y-shaped seed head, and it spreads by seeds and rhizomes. Bahia grass tends to be aggressive in nature, so it might be difficult to control where this grass grows. It is native to South America and was first introduced to the United States in Florida in 1913.

Centipede grass

Another low-maintenance grass, centipede grass spreads quickly; tolerates drought; resists weeds and pests; and requires little mowing, watering, or fertilizing. The main disadvantage of centipede grass is it does not tolerate foot traffic well. However, if you do not have children or will not otherwise use the lawn frequently for outdoor activities, this is one of the best grasses for individuals who do not have a lot of time to spend on lawn maintenance.

This course-textured perennial spreads by stolons and features short, upright stems that resemble centipedes, how this grass earned its name. Centipede grass prefers sandy, acidic soils in areas that receive more than 40 inches of rain annually. Although it can tolerate shady areas, it prefers full sunlight. Unlike other grasses, it does not enter a true dormant stage during the winter, and hard freezes can kill leaves and young stolons.

Zoysia

Zoysia is a slow-growing, thick grass and one of the only warm-weather grasses that does well in the south and also further north in some cool season and transitional areas. It requires less mowing than some of the faster-growing grasses such as St. Augustine and Bermuda and tolerates foot traffic well. It is drought tolerant and disease and insect resistant. Zoysia grass prefers growing in temperatures between 80 and 90 degrees, and it is considered the most cold tolerant of all warm-season grasses.

It prefers sun, but it is fairly shade tolerant and can grow in rocky, sandy, or poor soils with a pH between 5.8 and 7.5. Once the lawn is established, zoysia will need little water. It is best to wait until the blades of grass wilt slightly and then provide the lawn with ¾ inch water. Watering in this way will help the grass become more drought tolerant and will help the plant develop a deep root system. Because it is known to grow densely, zoysia can have problems with thatch, so homeowners with this type of grass will need to aerate their lawns in the spring and fall.

Transitional grasses

Because of the wide range of temperatures, neither cool nor warm season grasses do well in the transitional areas of the United

States; though, a mix of fescues tend to work well here because of the variety of conditions they can withstand. On the other hand, the best choices are native grasses to this country.

Buffalo grass

Buffalo grass, a true prairie grass, can be found in Texas, as well as the plains regions of the Midwest and West. Green to blue-green in color, it is extremely drought tolerant and can survive on little nitrogen. Buffalo grass requires little maintenance and will die if it is over-watered or fertilized or mowed too often. It works best in transitional areas that have between 15 and 30 inches of rainfall per year.

Do not plant Buffalo grass in areas that have heavy traffic or experience significant shade. The turf is thin and requires little mowing. If you decide to start this grass from seed, it is best to chill the seeds at 5 to 10 degrees for six to eight weeks before you plant them to allow them to germinate most successfully. It is best to plant Buffalo grass in April and May.

Little bluestem

Another prairie grass, little bluestem grows in clumps and, as its name implies, is blue-green in color. It is also drought tolerant and requires little mowing. Because it tends to brown during the cold season, manufacturers often mix it with hard fescue to ensure a green lawn during the winter months. Bluestem grows well on well-drained, medium to dry soils with a pH of 7.0 or higher. This grass often pairs well with wildflowers, often turns bright red in autumn, and features fluffy seedstalks. It can reach up to 4 feet in height and is mostly found in the Great Plains.

The following tables will help you choose the best grass or mix of grasses for your lawn based on climate; level of maintenance required; water requirement; tolerance to foot traffic; and heat, cold, and shade tolerance.

Climate/ Grass Type	Maintenance Requirement			Water Requirement			Tolerance to Foot Traffic		
	High	Medium	Low	High	Medium	Low	High	Medium	Low
Cool Season									
Kentucky bluegrass	X			X			X		
Perennial ryegrass			X	X			X		
Turf-type tall fescues			X			X		X	
Creeping red fescue			X			X		X	
Chewings fescue			X			X			X
Hard fescue			X			X			X
Warm Season									
Bermuda	X				X			X	
St. Augustine	X				X			X	
Bahia			X			X		X	
Centipede			X			X			X
Zoysia		X				X		X	
Transitional									
Buffalo			X			X		X	
Little bluestem			X			X		X	

Climate/ Grass Type	Heat Tolerance			Cold Tolerance			Shade Tolerance		
	High	Medium	Low	High	Medium	Low	High	Medium	Low
Cool Season									
Kentucky bluegrass			X	X			X		
Perennial ryegrass		X			X		X		
Turf-type tall fescues		X			X			X	
Creeping red fescue			X		X			X	
Chewings fescue		X			X		X		
Hard fescue		X			X			X	
Warm Season									
Bermuda	X				X				X
St. Augustine		X				X		X	
Bahia		X				X	X		
Centipede		X			X			X	
Zoysia		X			X			X	
Transitional									
Buffalo grass	X				X				X
Little bluestem		X			X				X

Remember, if you need more guidance, you can always ask your local Cooperative Extension Service, nursery, or garden center for help.

Do not become overwhelmed with the grass options available to you. Take the time to understand what options you have for your area. Talk to the local garden center to see the varieties. With the right grass and the right compost in the soil, you can create a strong foundation for your new grass. The next component of the organic lawn care process is fertilization, the process of adding additional nutrients to the soil and grass.

CASE STUDY:
JEFF SWANO

Jeff Swano
Dig Right In Landscaping, Inc™
President/Owner
jeff@digrightin.com
www.digrightin.com

Jeff Swano is owner of Dig Right In Landscaping. The company specializes in earth friendly landscaping in the Chicago area. Its mission since 1998 has been to create great looking, well-maintained lawns using organic processes. Swano provided some insight into his business services and inspirations.

"I am an environmental economist by schooling and my first 20 years of my career," he says. "I am also a gardener and naturalist. So, I understand how nature works, and I understand how chemicals are detrimental, from production to transport to application."

Swano compares the organic lawn care process to feeding a person. He says, "Just like eating healthily requires educating ourselves on the various food options available, healthy living practices require less exposure to toxic chemicals and learning about the subject matter. Thus, the 'green' revolution is actually a 'gray matter' revolution."

Swano is passionate about his services and believes using chemicals has led to soil sterilization, noting the biological activity in the soil is nearly gone. In order to fix this, Swano says, "The idea is to repopulate the soil with the entire soil food web so that the soil is manufacturing the fertilization necessary for plant health. Have you ever seen anyone out fertilizing the prairie or the woods? No, because a healthy soil food web exists in these ecosystems. As we repopulate the soil, imagine a day when no application of fertilizers is needed."

Being able to create a green lawn on your own is possible, but you need to have enough technical knowledge about the ecosystem that occurs in the soil. Swano shared his strategy for doing this:

"The strategy basically is:

> Take soil samples to know what fertilization and amendments it actually needs.

> Establish and increase the soil ecology primarily by applying compost tea. This includes all kinds of microorganisms, fungi, and predatory insects.

> Mow the grass higher to shade out weed seeds. Core-aerate twice per year.

> Overseed the lawn often to jam-pack it with turfgrass — eliminating bare spots.

> Water deeply to grow a deeper turfgrass root system. If watering is a problem in your area, do not be grow water-dependent turfgrass — seek an alternative species of grass to use.

> Use mechanical methods — pulling, forking — to get rid of weeds.

> Know the life cycle of bad insects and weeds and respond accordingly.

When dandelions populate a lawn in spring, homeowners reach for the broadcast herbicide. Once applied, the plant immediately goes into a defensive mode and actually goes to seed. The homeowner sees the dead leaves, but the plant has just won by sending out the next generation of seeds."

This is not the way to manage a lawn, and Swano offers the following solution. "The same effort to bend over and spray a weed can be accomplished with a weeding fork, as long as the lawn is not too far gone. If a lawn is too far gone with weeds, has poor soil, or has been overapplied with chemicals or other improper care issues, then starting over is the easiest way to go organic."

In some situations, it is necessary for homeowners to start a lawn from scratch because of the poor soil quality present. If that is the case, Swano offers the following advice. "To start over, remove the weeds and poor grass ,and evaluate the soil. Next, add compost and other organic sources of nutrients that are actually needed. Then, install some of the newer strains of sod available, such as rhizomatous tall fescue — which has deeper roots, has greater drought resistance, and is 'self-repairing' — so the customer has thick lawn right away. Organic care from that point is easy by following the strategy."

One of the problems many people deal with when it comes to creating an organic lawn is developing the lawn without care. However, turning to organic lawn care companies is difficult. When asked how to know if you can trust a company, Swano says, "You don't, and there is a lot of 'green-washing' going on out there. You have to know the overall strategy, read up a little on the techniques and products available, and then interview the service provider. Ask tough questions, particularly how the products actually work in the environment to achieve their results. Basically, if they are touting quick results, it most likely is not organic. As with all-natural functions, nature takes its course. Farmers can't rush the harvest."

What makes his business different from others? "We manufacture our own compost tea at our warehouse in Brookfield, Illinois. Talk about a small carbon footprint: Our main feedstock is compost, usually taken from my yard. We add additional organic compounds using a formulation made by a producer in Wisconsin and water."

Chapter 4

ORGANIC FERTILIZERS

The third ingredient in the foundation upon which you will build your organic lawn consists of the nutrients grass needs to grow strong and healthy and the organic fertilizers that contain them. These nutrients reside in the soil in which grass grows, and you can determine their amounts through soil testing. When nutrients are lacking, you can amend the soil by adding specific organic fertilizers that contain them.

Therefore, before describing the various organic fertilizers that you can apply to your lawn, it is important to first learn what these nutrients are and their effect on grass health. With a sound understanding of plant nutrition under your belt, you will be able choose the right organic fertilizers in the right amounts to improve the health of your soil, which will in turn improve the health of your grass.

Basic Nutrients Required for Healthy Soil and Grass

There are 16 elements, three nonminerals and 13 minerals that are essential to plant growth and health. Plants obtain the three nonmineral elements, oxygen, carbon, and hydrogen, from water and air. These three elements make up about 95 percent of the plant's structure. They get the 13 mineral elements, which represent the remaining 5 percent of a plant's structure, from the soil through their roots.

These 16 elements can be further classified on the basis of the amounts plants need to survive and thrive. Plants require macronutrients in large quantities and micronutrients in limited amounts. You are probably familiar with the three primary macronutrients, nitrogen, phosphorus, and potassium, which are the only ingredients to which most synthetic fertilizers can boast. These macronutrients represent 75 percent of the mineral nutrients plants contain.

There are also three secondary macronutrients: calcium, magnesium, and sulfur. Although plants require more of the primary macronutrients than they do the secondary ones, this does not mean you should exclude these secondary macronutrients or the micronutrients from a plant's diet as many synthetic fertilizer products often do. You will see in the following description of these lesser-required elements just how important they are to your organic lawn's overall health and vitality. Knowing what each of these nutrients does and knowing where and when to add these elements is an important part of a more complete and detailed organic lawn care program.

Nonmineral Macronutrients

Oxygen

Plants are composed of about 45 percent oxygen, the gas they exhale as waste. Plants receive oxygen from either water or air. Oxygen is the "ate" part of the word "carbohydrate" and bonds with carbon within the skeleton of the plant.

Carbon

Forty-four percent of a plant's structure is composed of carbon, an element found in all living organisms. Plants get carbon from the air in the form of carbon dioxide, the gas humans exhale. Plants retain the carbon from carbon dioxide and exhale the oxygen.

Hydrogen

Hydrogen, derived from water, represents about 6 percent of a plant's composition. It is the "hydro" part of the word "carbohydrate." Like oxygen, hydrogen bonds with carbon in the skeleton of the plant.

Oxygen, carbon, and hydrogen work together with sunlight in a process known as photosynthesis that produces the carbohydrates or simple sugars, starches, and cellulose, as well as amino acids, proteins, and enzymes plants need to grow. The remaining 13 elements, which make up the mineral macro and micronutrients, are listed in order of the most to the least amount grass needs to grow.

Primary Mineral Macronutrients

These primary nutrients are the basic building blocks of any quality organic lawn. The nutrients provide the stable base necessary for healthy growth.

Nitrogen

Nitrogen is the most common gas found in the earth's atmosphere. It is produced as a result of soil decomposition and is available to plants via their root system. Plants also absorb nitrogen from the atmosphere. It is the element most responsible for accelerated plant growth; it is an essential component of photosynthesis and produces proteins, enzymes, and chlorophyll; and it is responsible for blade growth and seed development.

Plants love nitrogen so much they will absorb more than they can handle in a balanced manner. Although the excess nitrogen produces more and greener grass, the grass itself is weak and more susceptible to disease. When grass absorbs nitrogen through the natural decay of organic matter found in soil fortified with compost, it absorbs the nitrogen and other nutrients more slowly than if it were included in artificial fertilizers, which in turn ensures the long-term health and stability of your lawn.

Phosphorus

Phosphorus is naturally found in soil and is responsible for converting light into the chemical energy needed for root formation, blooming, and seed growth. Phosphorus is an essential part of such chemical processes as photosynthesis, respiration, and the synthesis, or change, of fatty acids. These processes help the plant to gain necessary nutrients and turn those nutrients into energy it can use to grow and reproduce.

Potassium

Potassium is found in soil as a salt and helps plants resist disease. It also helps improve plant strength and resilience. Potassium ensures grass blades retain water, thereby helping them develop a greater resistance to drought.

Secondary Mineral Macronutrients

These mineral macronutrients will help balance the acidity and help stimulate growth.

Calcium

Calcium is one of the most important elements found within the walls of plant cells and helps stabilize soil pH levels. Found in topsoil and at levels all the way down to the bedrock, calcium is also responsible for transporting and retaining the elements within a plant's structure, and it helps strengthen plants.

Magnesium

Magnesium is a major element found in chlorophyll, which makes it crucial to photosynthesis. A naturally occurring mineral in the soil, magnesium helps keep particles of soil packed tightly together. It also is involved in activating many plant enzymes necessary for healthy plant growth.

Sulfur

Sulfur is an important element in the production of amino acids and proteins. It promotes chlorophyll formation and aids in the growth of seeds and root structure. Sulfur helps plants resist the damage low temperatures can cause.

Micronutrients

These are the nutrients that need to be used and balanced in providing for your lawn. Each of these micronutrients will play a different role and provide something different.

Boron

Boron helps produce grass seeds, carbohydrates, and sugars. You will find it in soil and manure.

Chlorine

Chlorine stabilizes organic matter and is crucial to ionic bonding and osmosis. It is used all over the world as a disinfectant. Most types of soil contain it in small amounts.

Copper

Copper is an element found in chlorophyll and is a necessary component of photosynthesis. It also has important functions in root formation and utilizing proteins. Copper also assists in plant reproduction.

Iron

Iron is an important catalyst in chlorophyll formation. Most types of soils contain it, and it is necessary for photosynthesis. It also acts as a carrier of oxygen.

Manganese

Manganese is necessary for chlorophyll production, as well as photosynthesis. Manganese is also involved in carbohydrate breakdown and helps plants use nitrogen. The amount of manganese found in soils varies widely.

Molybdenum

Molybdenum helps construct amino acids by being a **coenzyme factor** — a substance that needs to be present along with an enzyme so a certain reaction can take place. It also helps the plant use nitrogen and helps with pollen formation.

Zinc

Zinc is an essential element in carbohydrate formation, which helps to regulate sugar consumption. It is also a required catalyst in many important enzyme reactions that regulate plant growth. Zinc also aids in seed formation.

Types of Organic Fertilizers

Organic fertilizers contain the 13 mineral elements found in the soil that plants need to grow strong and healthy. They can be categorized on the basis of the source from which they are obtained: plants, minerals, and animals. A detailed soil test will reveal the nutrient levels in your soil and not only recommend organic sources for nutrients that are deficient, but also indicate how much of each to apply.

Plant-based Fertilizers

Although animal-based materials such as manure, blood, and bone meal have been used as the primary source of organic fertilizers for various types of agriculture and gardening needs, many homeowners prefer plant-based alternatives. People used fertilizers from plant sources — grains, water, and land plants — on lawns and gardens for centuries. There are a vast number of reasons for the exclusive use of plant-based fertilizers, but the main reason is simple: Manure and dead animal products are far more toxic and potentially harmful than plant-based fertilizers. Plant-based fertilizers are also far less expensive to acquire, and you can find them more commonly in nature. This makes them not only friendly to the environment but also practical.

Alfalfa meal

Alfalfa is a cool season perennial legume, which means it comes from the same family as beans and peanuts (legume), likes colder weather, and lives longer than two years. It is one of the most widely used plants in the world; it is harvested, cut into hay, and fed to beef and dairy cattle. The main reason for using alfalfa meal in organic lawn care is its high protein content as well as its generous fiber levels. It is grown all over the world in numerous climates, and the United States is its main producer, especially the states of California, South Dakota, and Wisconsin. One of the fascinating things about alfalfa is its ability to grow just about anywhere its stubborn little seeds are planted. This plant does so well because it grows such a deep root system, extending down as much as 15 feet, which makes it extremely drought resistant. It can grow in extremely cold regions, but you can also find it springing up in deserts.

Alfalfa makes an effective fertilizer because manufacturers process it into pellets easily distributed on the lawn. There are several places you can find this product, including a regular store, a nursery, a co-op, a farmers market, or an alfalfa meal distributor with its own website. There is no shortage of suppliers when it comes to alfalfa meal, just like there is no shortage of alfalfa.

Make sure to use the pellets as a fertilizer, not the regular hay or alfalfa plant itself, though alfalfa hay does make a great raw material for the compost bin. When alfalfa is converted into pellets, its nitrogen level increases, thus creating an effective, environmentally friendly means of increasing a lawn's nitrogen levels. Alfalfa in pellet form also makes it easier to distribute over your lawn using a fertilizer spreader.

Alfalfa meal is one of the best fertilizers you can obtain for your yard. It is composed of about 3 to 4 percent nitrogen. Another factor to consider is the nutrients in alfalfa meal are slow releasing and are good for long-term fertilization. Alfalfa also contains about 2 percent of potassium and less than 1 percent of magnesium, phosphorus, and sulfur, which are nutrients plants will benefit from as well. Alfalfa contains anywhere from 7 to 9 percent of calcium, making it one of the few organic fertilizers this calcium rich.

Corn gluten meal

Corn gluten is a miraculous substance that is a great nitrogen-rich fertilizer. It also serves as an effective organic herbicide. It eliminates weeds by not allowing the root structure of new plants to develop while leaving grass roots unharmed. Corn gluten is a byproduct of corn processing and has been used for decades to feed livestock. You can purchase it at many of the same places where you find alfalfa meal and other organic lawn care materials. Farm supply stores and garden centers will almost always carry it, and there are many online sources as well. *See the Resource Directory at the end of the book for a list of online sources where you can buy these materials.* You can buy it either as a powder or granules that can be mixed with water and made into a paste for certain types of application. When purchased as pellets, you can easily spread it on your lawn.

Although corn gluten does not contain five of the six macronutrients, it is extremely rich in nitrogen and contains about 10 percent, which is just as high or higher than many animal-based products. Do not use corn gluten on brand new lawns because it prevents newly sprouting grass from developing roots. It is only effective on already-established lawns.

Cottonseed meal

Cottonseed meal comes from crushed cottonseeds that no longer contain any oil. The primary concern with this material is the high amount of pesticides people spray on cotton crops in the United States and elsewhere. When shopping for this product, make sure you are purchasing a pesticide-free sample. If the label does not state it is free of pesticides, it will almost definitely contain them. You can purchase cottonseed meal from most feed stores.

Cottonseed reduces the pH levels and makes a great fertilizer for plants that prefer acidic soils. Although the nitrogen levels run somewhere around 7 to 8 percent as in most high-quality organic fertilizers, it also has phosphorus levels at around 2 to 3 percent. The potassium content is somewhere between 1 and 2 percent, and though the other three macronutrients — calcium, magnesium, and sulfur — register at less than 1 percent, they are at least present in trace amounts. Cottonseed meal can also help loosen tightly compacted soils and can help sandy mixtures retain more water. It helps plants develop strong root systems. When you use cottonseed meal on your lawn, add enough water so it penetrates the ground at least 2 inches below the surface in order to provide the most benefit to the plant.

Seaweed

Seaweed is a microorganism found in bodies of water around the world, and there are more than 10,000 species including algae and kelp. Gardeners in Scotland, England, and surrounding areas have used this product with great success and have created enormously lush lawns and bountiful gardens. Many inhabitants of the coastal areas of New England swear their miraculous plant growth is due to seaweed alone.

Any seaweed gathered by hand should be thoroughly rinsed with fresh water to reduce the salt content. Salt is not beneficial for plants when it is in soil. Many artificial fertilizers contain high levels of salts that damage the soil's ability to sustain plant life.

Many nurseries and farm supply stores, as well as other organic product outlets, sell different kinds of seaweed. Most of these varieties have a low salt content and receive processing, so the soil easily accepts it. Many online vendors, such as AlgaeGreen™ (**http://algaegreen.net**) and Eden Foods® (**www.edenfoods.com**) will ship seaweed right to your front door.

The nutrient content of seaweed is stunning. It is known to contain every one of the 16 elements essential to plant life. Seaweed boasts a potassium content of 4 to 6 percent and includes copper, molybdenum, iron, boron, zinc, manganese, and chlorine. In addition, most seaweeds contain mannitol, a chelating compound — a compound used to soften water — and alginate, which helps the soil hold water. Because the nitrogen and phosphorus levels in seaweed fertilizers are fairly low, they can provide a great source of nutrients without raising the nitrogen levels to an amount that could potentially harm a lawn.

Two of the most fascinating substances found within seaweed are cytokinin and auxin. Even though the ideal ratio between these compounds has yet to be discovered, it is known that the higher the amount of cytokinin, the faster the above-ground region of the plant will grow, and the higher the amount of auxin, the faster the root system will grow. Discovering the best ratio of these two compounds has been of particular interest to many turfgrass managers in recent years. Research suggests cytokinin promotes cell division (mitosis), while auxin acidifies the newly created cell walls and allows for the new growth to occur. The result is grass that grows stronger and more quickly. Enhanced drought resistance and root growth are two more important benefits of cytokinin and auxin.

Soybean meal

Soybean meal is created from the flakes of soybeans that have had most of the oil removed. It can be purchased in the same locations as alfalfa, corn gluten, and cottonseed meal, including through online retailers and most organic garden centers. Like cottonseed meal, soybean meal reduces soil pH levels, making it another excellent choice for acid-loving grasses. Its nutrient content is nearly identical to cottonseed meal except for the slightly higher levels of phosphorus, which are somewhere between 2 and 3 percent. The primary advantage of soybean meal is its heavy protein content. It is in pellet form and thus is another fertilizer easily applied to your lawn with a fertilizer spreader.

Wood ash

Unlike seaweed, which is only locally available to coastal residents, wood ash is available to anyone who burns wood in a fireplace or anyone who regularly uses wood as fuel for the barbecue pit. Wood ash can also be found at online sources such as Amazon.com® (**www.amazon.com**) and eBay® (**www.ebay.com**). Local restaurants that regularly use a wood grill are another potential source of this organic fertilizer. Wood ash has no nitrogen, but it does have decent phosphorus levels — about 2 percent — and a whopping 6 percent potassium. Although there is little, if any, sulfur and only about 1 to 2 percent magnesium in wood ash, it has an astoundingly high volume of calcium — 20 percent or more.

Remember that wood ash is meant as a fertilizer primarily for acidic soils that have a low pH level. Adding it to soil that has a high pH level will increase its alkalinity. Make sure to test your soil's pH level before applying wood ash.

Mineral-based Fertilizers

Minerals are naturally occurring substances found in the earth that are the building blocks of rocks. When rocks are crushed, the minerals contained in the sand and dust can be applied to the lawn to increase its mineral content. The 13 macro and micronutrients plants need to grow are all minerals. A benefit of using minerals to fortify your lawn is these nutrients release slowly; some take months to be fully released into the soil, which should spare you some expense. Apply these substances directly on the lawn, and add the substances to compost piles to help enrich the nutrient content of the compost.

None of the mineral-based materials mentioned in this chapter contain nitrogen. With the notable exception of rock phosphates and greensand, none of the mineral fertilizers contain any phosphorus. A soil test will tell you if and how much of these substances your soil may need.

Greensand

Greensand is a sandstone rock found in narrow bands of ancient mineral deposits all over the world. Since the 17th and 18th centuries, gardeners and horticulturalists have used greensand as a practical and natural organic solution to increase potassium levels. Greensand is mined in Texas, New Jersey, and Arkansas, as well as other countries around the world, such as England and Scotland. It is also known for its ability to loosen soils that have a high clay content.

The primary nutrient found in greensand is potassium, which is usually about 8 to 10 percent. Greensand also contains about 1 percent phosphorus and trace amounts of calcium, sulfur, and other micronutrients. The magnesium content is somewhere between 2 to 4 percent. Greensand is slightly basic with a pH of around 8.3. One of the more specialized aspects of greensand is its huge iron content that can be as high as 20 percent. If your soil is iron deficient, greensand is an organic option to consider.

Granite dust

The nutrients in granite dust are an inexpensive form of potassium enrichment, are slow releasing, and will not alter the pH levels of the soil. Granite has been used as a construction material in the Egyptian pyramids and other ancient structures for at least the last 6,000 years. It is sold at nurseries and garden centers. Many commercial lawn care companies will apply granite dust regularly in the fall as part of their annual potassium regimen. Many commercial fertilizers that manufacturers recommend for fall lawn application contain high doses of potassium, which promotes winter hardiness.

Gypsum

Gypsum is a mineral rich in calcium and sulfur. Benjamin Franklin used this rich organic substance as a fertilizer for his plants. It is used to help break up soils thick with clay and also provide a pH-neutral way to elevate calcium levels.

You can spread granular gypsum with a regular fertilizer spreader without any risk of toxic effects to children or pets, unlike some commercial synthetic fertilizers. Gypsum dissolves in water over time, and it is an environmentally friendly way to elevate soil's calcium and sulfur levels. Conduct a thorough soil test before using this product because even though a lawn may benefit from the extra calcium, if the sulfur content in the soil is already too high, it should not be used. Instead, use limestone as a calcium supplement because extreme sulfur levels can cause too much alkalinity, which is unhealthy for lawns. Gypsum also contains trace amounts of magnesium and potassium.

Phosphates

There are two kinds of phosphates used in lawn care: hard rock phosphates and soft — or colloidal — rock phosphates. The hard rock phosphates contain high amounts of calcium — sometimes 30 to 40 percent or more — and the soft rock phosphates contain 25 percent of phosphorus and 10 percent of sulfur, which is what makes rock phosphates so popular among organic gardeners. Soft rock phosphates are a phosphorus gold mine with only bonemeal, an animal-based organic fertilizer, as its nearest rival. If a soil is low in phosphorus and the sulfur content is not too high, use rock phosphates instead of bonemeal. If the sulfur content is already high, consider bonemeal as an organic alternative. Soft rock phosphates also contain several micronutrients in addition to their phosphorus and sulfur content.

Limestone

Limestone is a mineral also known as calcium carbonate. It is a sedimentary rock mined all over the world and is used for many types of buildings and structures. Manufacturers use it to create cement, mortar, quicklime, and slaked lime. These products have various uses, from construction applications to treating sewage in treatment plants.

Limestone raises the calcium levels in acidic soil. It contains a fairly decent amount of magnesium — dolomite limestone contains about 10 percent, and high-calcium limestone has around 2 to 4 percent of calcium. When the soil is alkaline and needs both magnesium and calcium, use dolomite limestone. High-calcium limestone also increases alkalinity, but use it in soil that has an adequate amount of magnesium. Trace amounts of potassium and sulfur are also present in the chemical structure of limestone.

Langbeinite

This commonly used potassium-magnesium-sulfate fertilizer receives its name from the 19th century German chemist A. Langbein. It consists of potassium (a little more than 20 percent), magnesium (18 percent), and sulfur (28 percent). The primary advantage for using langbeinite, which you can purchase at most garden centers and farm supply outlets, is it can add magnesium to alkaline soils without raising the pH levels. Once again, make sure to test your soil before using this product, because once you add it, its nutrient release will be slow. Make sure your soil needs magnesium added before you decide to apply it, and make sure you do not already have too high a sulfur content. There are other sources of magnesium that will not add so much sulfur to the soil if your sulfur levels are already high or adequate.

Zeolites

Zeolites are primarily beneficial as **adsorbents**, substances that can collect a liquid, gas, or dissolved substance on their surfaces. People have used zeolites in many European countries to prevent nutrients from leaching from sandy soils. This mineral substance contains approximately 3 percent potassium and 3 percent calcium, which slowly release into the soil without altering the pH level.

Animal-based Fertilizers

Fertilizers from animal sources should be applied with great care and only if there is no plant- or mineral-based alternative available because many of these substances are considered toxic. You certainly do not want to use them on your lawn if you intend it as a play area for your children and pets because these animal-based fertilizers contain remnants of dead and decaying animal parts and waste.

Although farmers may have used manure to fertilize their crops, the nutrient content of manure, contrary to popular belief, is not that outstanding. In fact, most types of excrement do not offer 1 percent of any of the primary and secondary macronutrients. Dead animal parts and waste also emit a foul odor, so think carefully before applying it to your lawn. The two nontoxic and odor-free, animal-based fertilizers you can add to your lawn are bonemeal and vermicompost.

Animal-based fertilizers do have some nutrient value. You can apply this fertilizer safely if the right precautions are taken to keep from coming into direct contact with them. Be sure to wear sturdy gloves and shoes, as well as clothes that will protect your arms and legs. After applying animal-based fertilizers on your lawn, it is a good idea to place a sign on your lawn explaining you have used animal-based products.

Manure

Although many people have used this substance as fertilizer, it is not that rich in nutrients. Only chicken manure has nitrogen levels that are more than 2 percent, and the nutrient levels in the other commonly used manure — cow, horse, and sheep — are less than 1 percent. Never apply manure directly to your lawn, as it may burn the grass. Instead, add it to your compost pile to dilute its strength over the decomposition time. Sterilized manure is available commercially from garden centers and even the grocery store. It is probably a better choice than fresh manure. Sterilization kills off weed seeds that might be introduced into your soil with fresh manure. Sterilized manure offers the same type of result as the nonsterilized manure.

Blood and feather meal

Blood meal is animal blood left over from the meat packing process that has been dried and made into a powdered form. Feather meal comes from cooking feathers, most often from chickens, with steam and pressure and then drying and grinding them into powder. Both of these meals are nitrogen rich — 12 to 15 percent or higher — and are slow-releasing fertilizers. Blood meal also contains about 3 percent phosphorus content. The pH level of blood and feather meal is low and acidic. You can purchase these products at most garden or farm supply stores.

Bonemeal

Bonemeal is one notable exception among all of the animal-based products and can be used without worry. It is not as likely to have toxic effects to the immediate environment as most of the other animal-based products. It is also one of the few fertilizers that has a high content of phosphorus and calcium — roughly 20 percent each; rock phosphates are the only other fertilizer that can make this claim. If there is a need for either of these critical elements, bonemeal makes an excellent source. It also contains a decent amount of nitrogen — about 4 percent — and trace amounts of magnesium and sulfur. Bone meal is a slow-release fertilizer, and its pH level is low and acidic, which makes it an even more attractive option if your soil is a bit too alkaline.

Fish products

Experts do not recommend fish products as organic fertilizers because of their smell and other safety issues. They have a lot of nitrogen — as much as 12 percent or more — while also offering 6 percent of calcium and phosphorus. They contain trace amounts of magnesium and sulfur as well. Because they are a slow-release fertilizer, fish products are acidic and have low pH levels.

Inoculants

A special category of soil amendments that have come into recent use are inoculants. Manufacturers add this bacteria to the soil in order to support processes such as feeding, disease resistance, and microbial activity. There are three popular types of inoculants widely available for consumer use: algae, mycorrhizae, and rhizobia. They have been used extensively and have well-documented histories of producing stunning results. These products deserve mention in any book about organic lawn care because they have had numerous positive results when applied and used correctly.

Algae

Spraying algae on the surface of the soil produces positive benefits. Because algae can help draw more nitrogen into the soil and helps reverse soil compaction, professional lawn-maintenance experts have used this organic inoculant for many years. This product is now widely available in many nurseries or garden supply stores.

Mycorrhizae

These beneficial fungi make their homes in or on a plant's roots and increase a plant's ability to absorb water and nutrients. This results in a faster rate of plant growth, as well as resistance to disease and pests. Several descriptions of the amazing results this fungus can produce can be found on the customer testimonial page of Mycorrhizal Applications, Inc.® at **http://mycorrhizae. com**. In addition to improving root systems, mycorrhizae has been shown to increase chlorophyll levels significantly. In order to use this inoculant effectively, you will need to aerate the soil sufficiently to allow the fungi to get to the root system of the lawn.

Rhizobia

The name "rhizobia" literally means "root life." These bacteria are found in legumes. They infiltrate the root systems and create nodules that help grass obtain nitrogen from the surrounding air. These beneficial fungi are naturally found on clover and are widely available from many sources all over the country. Rhizobia require a host plant and cannot survive independently because they are a parasitical fungi and do not have the necessary biological equipment to live on their own.

Your local Cooperative Extension Service or garden center should be able to answer any questions you may have about using inoculants on your lawn.

Chapter 5

EASY ORGANIC LAWN CARE

*F*or some, gardening is a great escape, a way to give back to nature in a quiet, peaceful way. But let's face it. Not everyone was blessed with a green thumb and the time to make gardens and yards beautiful. Never fear, busy would-be gardeners. This chapter outlines the ways you can cut down on the work associated with maintaining a lawn and still keep your lawn organic. Some of the tips provided in this chapter are endorsed by the USDA.

Even if you do not have a lot of time or money to spend caring for your lawn, you can implement an organic lawn through several steps. One advantage that organic lawn care has over traditional lawn care methods is it does not take nearly the amount of time and work that traditional methods require. This is because the bulk of what you will do is discontinuing many of the practices associated with traditional lawn care. Most of your time will be spent fertilizing, mowing, and watering the lawn, and these activities will not require much time, giving you more of it to spend enjoying your lawn with family and friends.

Another alternative to traditional lawn care you may not be familiar with **xeriscaping**. Xeriscaping is easy to implement and maintain. It uses grasses and other plants that require less water and places those plants in strategic methods to reduce the overall need for watering. Slopes and hills help plants requiring more water to get it. This is a landscaping method often used in parts of the country where water is scarce. It is also an excellent choice for individuals who may have a little extra money to spend to restructure the yard but lack the time required to maintain a grass lawn. In addition, though it may require an initial outlay of money and work, once it is completed, the labor required to maintain it is minimal.

Equipment and Supplies Needed

It does not take a lot of equipment and supplies to implement this organic lawn care option. At a minimum, you will need a lawn

mower, a garden hose, drum roller, and sprinklers. If you decide to fertilize your lawn with compost tea, you will need to make a batch. *See Chapter 2 for the instructions to make it.* Equipment and supplies needed for xeriscaping are discussed in this section.

Lawn mower

Lawn mowers come in several varieties and sizes. If you already own a lawn mower, it does not make sense to buy another one if the one you have does an adequate job of cutting your grass. However, if you do not own a lawn mower, there are several models to choose from based on the size of your yard, the amount of elbow grease you care to use, and how much money you have to spend.

The three types of lawn mowers are rotary mowers, reel mowers, and riding mowers.

- Rotary mowers are engine powered with flat, horizontal cutting blades attached to a shaft that is connected to the engine and sits on top of the mower covering. Gas,  electricity, or batteries power the engine. Electric rotary mowers are lightweight and require little maintenance, mostly blade sharpening. A disadvantage of these mowers is you have to plug a cord into an electric outlet to operate them. Gas mowers, on the other hand, are heavier and, therefore, harder to push and need the same kind of maintenance a car requires, including engine tuneups, oil changes, and gasoline to power it. Another disadvantage of gas-powered mowers is the pollution in the form of carbon emissions. With battery-powered mowers, your mowing time is a function of how long the batteries last, normally no more than 45 minutes. Their advantage lies in the fact that you do not have to worry about plugging a cord into an electric outlet.

Rotary mowers, whether gas, electric, or battery powered, are pushed, but many come with a self-propelled option that powers either the front or back wheels, reducing the amount of pushing you have to do. Rotary mowers also come with a mulching option, cutting grass clippings into mulch before releasing them onto the lawn where they decompose quickly and fertilize the lawn. A bagging option releases the grass clippings into a bag, which you can carry to your compost pile.

- The least expensive and lightest lawn mowers are reel mowers. These mowers have been around for a long time  and are great for use on small lawns. The blades attach to a revolving cylinder, which allows the blades to spin, thereby cutting the grass as the mower is pushed forward. Reel mowers do not tear the grass as rotary mowers do. They give the grass a clean, sharp cut, but the grass needs to stay at 3 inches or less; otherwise, it will be hard to push the mower. The major maintenance they require is blade sharpening, and you can have a lawn care professional do that for you. Reel mowers give you a great workout, they are nonpolluting, and they do not make nearly the amount of noise that rotary mowers do. Use this method if you plan to leave grass clippings in the grass. Otherwise, it is necessary to use a rake to clean the clippings up.

- If you can afford one and have a large lawn, you may want to consider a gas- or electric-powered riding  mower. In addition to mowing the lawn, it comes with attachments or carts you can hook up to the back of the mower for towing heavy items. They can be comfortable and easy to operate. The biggest disadvantage is their high cost — more than $1,000. They are also heavy and tend to compact the soil, leaving little room for air and water to circulate. Consult your lawn mower dealer for advice on whether this mowing option is worth the cost.

Hoses

Hoses for watering your lawn come in a variety of materials, length, and cost. The thicker a hose is — that is, the more "plies," or layers it has — the more expensive it will be.

Rubber hoses last longer than vinyl hoses, which tend to kink, crack, and leak where the hose attaches to the nozzle and water faucet. The best hose material is a combination of rubber and vinyl. The wider the diameter of the hose is, greater than ½ inch, the better to reduce watering time. Hose couplings, the metal ring at either end of the hose, should be made of brass because it is durable.

It is always a good idea to roll the hose up when not in use and either place it on a hanger or house it in a reel. Be sure to empty all the water out before rolling it up to prevent the water from becoming stagnant. Store the hose in a cool, dry space. Heat and sunlight will weaken the hose material and reduce the years of use it will give you.

Sprinklers

It takes a long time to water a large lawn with a garden hose, so investing in a sprinkler system is a good idea. Sprinklers water the lawn more effectively than hoses because the hose distributes the water in an even pattern over the lawn. But, the strength of their ability to circulate water across your lawn depends on how much water pressure they receive from the hose it attaches to.

There are several types of sprinklers to choose from, depending on how they distribute water over your lawn: fixed or stationary, spinning, oscillating, and impulse.

- Stationary or fixed sprinklers do not have any moving parts; they simply shoot water out of holes at the top of the sprinkler.

Many come with the option of covering the lawn in a specific pattern, such as a circle, rectangle, semicircle, or fan. Although they are inexpensive, you have to move them periodically to cover a large lawn. They also have a tendency to leak, and the holes can clog.

- Another sprinkler option for a small lawn is a spinning sprinkler. This inexpensive sprinkler works well on most lawns. The top nozzles of the sprinkler rotate quickly, allowing the water to shoot out of them in a fast motion. Many of these sprinklers sit on the ground, but some versions have a sharp, spear-shaped bottom to insert into the ground and extend up to 3 feet into the air. The value in a spinning sprinkler is the device can expel a significant amount of water over the surface of the lawn in a short amount of time, while creating a natural rainfall pattern. The nozzle holes can get clogged, though, and a poorly designed product is unlikely to withstand the necessary movements from one location to the next.

- An oscillating sprinkler is another version. These are perhaps the least expensive and are readily available.

 These are the most commonly used sprinkler because of how effective the device works. Most large oscillating sprinklers can cover an area as large as 20 to 30 feet. The spray ejects from the device in a fan-shaped curtain, which

shoots water to cover a 5- to 6-foot area. The metal arm of the oscillating sprinkler turns back and forth, normally at a slow pace, to mimic rainfall over the lawn. The biggest drawback of this type of sprinkler is you need to move the device from one section of the lawn to the next, unless the lawn is smaller than the device covers. It is not the most durable of sprinklers, but replacing this version is inexpensive.

- Impulse sprinklers are also called impact sprinklers. This irrigation sprinkler offers a long throw radius of between  20 and 41 feet. The water shoots out of the device and distributes evenly across the area, creating a natural rainfall effect in most cases. A higher-quality product will offer an even pattern and will work evenly. The sprinkler works by pivoting in a circular motion. The water sprays in intermittent streams of water, which creates a uniform waterfall effect. Because of their design, these sprinklers are more durable. In addition, new versions are constructed from thermoplastics, which have improved their resistance to corrosion.
Thermoplastics are a new type of plastic that is highly elastic and flexible.

Selecting the right sprinkler for your lawn does not have to be a hard decision. Pick your favorite within your budget. For those with more money to spend, consider investing in a stationary system that has a professional installation and remains in place all year. These water systems are the most effective way to get even water coverage to your lawn.

Watering your grass is a necessary step in caring for your lawn. When the right sprinkler, lawn mower, and hoses are used, the process is simplified. The next step you may have is putting together a plan to keep your grass looking great that does not require a lot of time or hard work in the process.

Drum roller

A drum roller can be a great tool to add to your lawn care arsenal. There are two primary types of these. The first one you will walk behind and push in order to flatten your lawn and to create a more even surface. The second type of drum roller is one in which you will be able to attach to a tractor and drag it behind you to flatten out your lawn as well.

Either option is an acceptable way to flatten out the lawn as part of the preparation procedures. Make sure when you use the drum roller you do not overfill or underfill the roller with sand or water. If you overfill the roller, you will end up creating ruts in the grass and will flatten all of your hard work. If you underfill the roller, you will end up doing little to no work of value to the lawn and will end up having to do it repeatedly.

Six Steps to Easy Lawn Care

Now that you have the equipment you need to build a strong and healthy lawn, the following steps will help you put together a plan of action. In this section, the goal is to create an easy system for caring for your lawn that does not focus on using chemicals or other inorganic treatments. By removing these products from your lawn care plan and focusing on the following steps, the lawn will look great and will be healthier for you, your family, and the lawn itself.

Stop using chemical fertilizers

What is wrong with using chemical fertilizers? They seem so simple to use. Visit the lawn and garden center, pick up a bag of fertilizer, use a spreader to spread it evenly, and the fertilizer does the work for you. Although that may not sound like a harmful process, it can be one of the worst things you can do for your lawn's health.

Whatever is put on the ground seeps into the water supply. Most fertilizers have a high nitrogen level, which flushes into local streams and waterways. It ends up in the water that comes out of your faucets. Your body does not need and cannot use such high levels of chemicals. In addition, water treatment centers cannot remove many of these chemicals from the water. They can lead to excessive growth in the plant life that grows underwater in the streams and waterways. This leads to hypoxia, a condition in which the level of oxygen in the water is so low that fish cannot survive.

To make matters even worse, lawns become dependent on fertilizers for their health. The sudden flush of green may make the lawn look brighter, but the lawn then becomes addicted to the chemicals, which leads to watering more frequently and needing to apply the chemicals more often to continue producing that healthy lawn look. This does not equate to an easy lawn care program.

You can solve this by making the decision to use only organic lawn fertilizers on your lawn. This will create a more natural look that is more appealing than a carpet of green. This is the simplest of the steps to beginning an organic lawn care program: stop using chemical-based fertilizers.

In addition to these harmful toxins, also avoid using pesticides and weed killers on your lawn. Those have the same effect as chemicals do on the water system and on your lawn in general. With proper lawn care, as depicted in this book, you simply will not need to apply pesticides or weed killers to your lawn.

Water less often

You will find that when you stop using fertilizers and allow your lawn to heal, you will need to use less water to care for it. Watering less often is better for the lawn because it encourages the lawn to develop deeper, stronger roots, which helps ensure each blade of grass is healthy. Most importantly, watering too much can be a significant problem.

First, the lawn's need for water depends on various factors, including the frequency of rain, how wet the soil already is, and the type of grass you have. When watering the lawn, the first few layers of soil need to be saturated. After that point, you are only wasting water if you continue to water the lawn. The water does not absorb any deeper into the ground than the first few inches.

Too much water can wash away nutrients in the soil that plants needs to grow and flourish. Over-watering can even lead to disease within the lawn, similar to what happens when plants get too much water.

It is best to limit watering to just three times per week, if needed. Set a rain gauge to monitor how much rain the lawn receives each week. Over-watering occurs when more than 1 inch of rain hits the lawn in any weekly period. Although grass needs differ, this is the general guideline to follow. All your lawn needs is about 1 inch of rain or watering. By cutting back on the amount of watering you do, you will improve the quality of your lawn rapidly.

Mow at a higher level and less often

Mowing your lawn may be one of your least favorite tasks to do. But, here is the good news — doing it less may be the ideal way to maintain your grass's health.

Mowing your grass at a higher level, which means allowing it to grow taller, will improve its quality and consistency. When grass remains taller, this improves the soil's moisture retention by blocking some of the evaporation. Mowing less often and keeping the grass at a higher level makes maintaining your lawn that much easier and keeps the grass looking thick and flush.

Keep the lawn mower's blade 3 or 4 inches off the ground. To keep grass looking greener, keep the blade higher throughout the year until September or the start of cooler weather in your area. At that time, drop it lower in preparation for the winter season.

Do not mow the lawn unless it is growing. Avoid mowing the lawn during a dry spell or when the lawn has stopped growing in the fall.

The taller grass will help to protect the soil because it offers a bit of shade to the soil. It also blocks out some types of weeds, such as crabgrass, from infiltrating the lawn itself. Crabgrass cannot gain sustenance when the lawn remains higher because it cannot reach the sun.

Leave after mowing

Although grass clippings drying on a newly mowed lawn may look tackier than you would like, think twice before removing them because grass clippings mean organic fertilizer.

What you are in fact doing when you leave grass clippings on the lawn is feeding your grasses. The clippings will break down over time, which allows the nutrients stored in the grass to be redeposited back into the lawn, creating a healthier soil. When you allow the clippings to remain in the grass, less fertilizer is necessary to keep the grass lush and beautiful.

In addition to this, the clippings help give the grass the full look many people desire. Rather than overseeding the lawn or using excessive fertilizer to encourage new growth for a thicker lawn, simply leave the clippings on the grass.

For better results, use a mulching lawn mower. This type of lawn mower minces the grass clippings into small pieces. When left in the grass, the clippings are barely noticeable. The smaller pieces allow decomposition to occur faster. This means the clippings return to fertilizer for the lawn faster, too.

Fertilize with compost tea

If your lawn shows signs of nutrient deficiency — brown spots — but you are not prepared to get the soil tested and amend it with organic fertilizers, spraying it with compost tea can go a long way toward improving the soil and strengthening the grass.

Compost tea works like a bath of nutrients. It is one of the best solutions for nourishing a lawn deficient in the nutrients needed to flourish. Compost tea is not something you need to use frequently. Use it as a tool to restore your lawn to a healthy state after you stop using chemical fertilizers or when the lawn is otherwise in need of nutrient enrichment.

Stop trying to keep up with the Joneses

It is a common problem in today's suburbs. Individuals want to do everything they can to have a great looking lawn, just as their neighbors do. Often, as soon as the snow is gone, homeowners take to their yards, trying to spruce them up in an effort to have the most beautiful or the most well-kept lawn in the neighborhood.

Even though it is important for homeowners to take the time to care for their lawn, it is not necessary to overdo it. So far in this chapter, you have learned several ways to reduce the amount of time spent caring for your lawn, such as not over-watering or overcutting the lawn. In addition to this, restrict yourself from overcaring for the lawn.

Those who try to keep up with the neighbors are more likely to incorporate inorganic lawn care products into the lawn care plan because these products offer a boost of color or fullness that takes longer to achieve with organic products. In the long term, however, the health of lawn is better if you use only organic products.

If you spend more time focusing on your own lawn care and disregard what your neighbors do, the overall quality of your lawn will improve to far better levels than what the neighbors are doing using chemical-based treatments and fertilizers.

Can Xeriscaping Work for You?

In an effort to focus on easy lawn care methods that cut down on the amount of time you spend landscaping, consider xeriscaping. This method of lawn care initially takes intense planning and work to implement, but once complete, the lawn and the garden will take care of itself for the most part. Xeriscaping is not necessarily the right option for everyone because it does require installing a new landscaping design. It also may require investing in new products, including new grasses and landscaping pieces, to create the overall look.

You will take steps in this method of gardening to reduce the frequency and need to water. Xeriscaping is an ideal solution for those areas where a water supply is not readily available and in situations where individuals wish to avoid watering a lawn.

In xeriscaping, the goal is to reduce the amount of water used overall. This is a form of creating a water-conserving, drought-tolerant landscape. Sometimes, people call it smartscaping because it allows gardeners to better use one of the world's most limited resources: fresh water. The goal here is to have a great looking lawn that does not need a lot of water to flourish.

Xeriscaping benefits

When done properly, a landscape using this method will require little or no watering because the plants and the landscaping design allow for the best water retention and the smallest need for water. In terms of the lawn itself, you will not need to mow it. That may be the biggest savings to anyone using this method of lawn care. In addition, there is little need to use any fertilizers on the lawn or on the other plants in the landscape design, including organic fertilizers. As you can imagine, this can cut down on your costs considerably. This is even more affordable than using all organic fertilizing.

In addition to all of these factors, xeriscaping is also one of the best options for the environment as a whole. It does not require irrigation, which means it does not deplete the water already available in the environment. Without fertilizers and mowing, you cut back on the harmful effects these actions cause on the environment.

Overall, the advantages of using this particular type of lawn and garden landscaping include reducing the need for consuming imported water or using ground water. You will put less time and effort into maintaining the landscaping. Those who may not enjoy gardening or who need a less stressful form of gardening will benefit the most from this type of landscaping. In addition, with the right selection of plants and implementing the right design, soil grading, and mulching, you can retain enough rainfall to sustain all aspects of the landscape. The plants thrive in this environment.

Before deciding if xeriscaping is the right option for you, consider the process of designing and implementing this type of landscaping in your garden and yard. It may not be the right choice for your particular goals if you are looking for a lush, green lawn.

Designing and maintaining a xeriscaped lawn

Xeriscaping is an excellent tool for those who are starting fresh with a new lawn or those who have the ability to make significant changes to the lawn. There are several key principles of effective xeriscaping. The basics are listed here, but for those who are considering investing in xeriscaping, it is often best to use a professional service to install the lawn.

Planning and design

The first consideration is the plan and design of the lawn. Create a diagram of the lawn and outline all major elements of the yard, including where existing trees, structures, and walkways are located. Select the locations for specific types of landscaping, including where perennial beds, turf, and slopes will be located. The key here is to focus on ways to reduce water needs, such as placing plants requiring more surface water at the bottom of a slope.

Soil amendment

Using organic fertilizers only, the next step for the landscaper is to amend the soil, normally using compost. The compost material not only nourishes the plants and the lawn, but it also helps the soil to retain water longer.

Efficient irrigation

Irrigation is part of a xeriscaping plan, but implement it into the landscape with an automatic sprinkler system. This will save time and effort because you no longer need to stand and water the lawn. This system uses numerous types of irrigation to accommodate the specific needs of the landscape, including drip lines, sprayers, and bubblers. **Drip irrigation** is the process of applying water directly to the roots of the plant in a slow dripping process to maintain optimum moisture in the soil. **Sprayers** spray water over an area, allowing the water to seep into the soil similar to how rain would. **Bubblers** are small sprinkler heads that dispense water at a slow rate and for a small area rather than for an entire garden. The grass will do best using rotary spray nozzles or gear driven rotors for use.

In terms of irrigation, the goal is to water deeply and evenly but to water infrequently. This allows the deeper roots of the grass and other plants to develop further. Water in the evening to reduce the amount lost to evaporation. Use a rain sensor to turn off automatic sensors when the weather conditions are more favorable. Some automatic sprinkler systems come equipped with a rain sensor, a device that alerts the sprinkler system to the amount of rain received. Then, the sprinkler system can adjust the amount of watering it does to the lawn.

Selecting the right plants

The next important principle of xeriscaping is selecting appropriate plants. Select plants based on the conditions in the yard and the natural design of the land. Some areas of the yard will receive more wind, light, and moisture naturally. Group plants together that have the same requirements of water and sunlight. Place those plants in areas where the landscape meets the plant's requirements best.

For the lawn itself, selecting varieties of grass that require less water is important. It may be possible or necessary to invest in different types of grass for separate areas of the space to ensure the area can sustain the type of grass planted.

Mulching

Mulching is just as important as composting. For the grass itself, mulching is not as significant. However, as part of a xeriscaping plan, incorporate mulching in any area where the landscaper places plants, such as in flowerbeds or near trees and shrubs. Two to 4 inches of mulch is best. Mulching minimizes the amount of water lost to evaporation, reduces the weeds that grow, and improves the health of the root systems. It also stops the soil from crusting and becoming difficult to use.

Organic mulches are a good option for any area. Using inorganic mulches, such as gravel and rocks, is helpful especially around driveways and walkways. Rock does heat the soil more so than other mulches, so limit the number of plants placed near the rocks because the rocks cause water to evaporate faster.

Alternative turf

Bluegrass and other traditional varieties of grasses are not good options for xeriscaping because these types of grasses need more water on a regular basis. Replacing these are alternative turf lawns. These types of turf require about one quarter of the amount of water traditional bluegrass requires. The most common turfs for xeriscaping are Buffalo grass and blue grama grasses, which are native grasses rather than cultivated varieties. During the warm season, such as June through September throughout much of the United States, these grasses are a deep green color. During the rest of the year, the grasses turn a straw brown color. Although they look dead, the grasses are simply conserving water and nutrients during these periods.

Other native grasses, called cool season grasses, are much different. These are greenest during the fall and spring months and are dormant during the summer months when heat is at its peak. These varieties include Reveille and tall fescue. These consume about 30 percent less water than traditional bluegrass varieties. Selecting the right grass for your lawn is critical in xeriscaping because this defines the amount of water needed to maintain the lawn.

Maintenance

The final principle of xeriscaping is maintenance. Although xeriscaping cuts down on the amount necessary, there is always some care required. Turf grasses will need aeration during the fall and spring months to allow oxygen to penetrate the soil, and fertilizing with organic fertilizers is necessary every two to three months. Do not remove clippings from the lawn, but do use a mulching lawn mower on these grasses, which shreds the grass clippings into small pieces so the clippings decompose faster. Other plants, including trees, shrubs, and perennials, will need pruning and removal of dead plant material. Replacing compost and mulch may also be necessary.

Those utilizing xeriscaping are likely to have a beautiful lawn and garden that require far less work and overall maintenance. This process can be extensive at first, but once in place, it can serve your needs ideally. The steps and tips included in this chapter outline the specifics of making organic lawn care simplistic so anyone can get started. This is why this book looks at how to get your organic lawn started from the beginning.

Chapter 6

STARTING AN ORGANIC LAWN FROM SCRATCH

*I*n a perfect world, your lawn would provide plants with optimal soil, water, and sunlight, and it would already contain only the healthy nutrients it needs to thrive. This is rarely the case today.

In this chapter, the focus is on starting an organic lawn from scratch. This is ideal for those just moving into a new construction site or those who may have a natural landscape. In the next chapter, the goal is to rehabilitate a lawn from its current state of chemical toxicity to a healthy, organic lawn. This is a recommendation of the USDA to help improve lawn care overall. The two processes are different in terms of timetables, costs, and overall expectations of the lawn.

Starting a lawn from scratch has benefits, including the following:

- There is no need to worry about removing chemicals from the pre-existing grass.

- You can select the type of grass you would like and place it where you want to put it.

- It can be more economical in the long term to start with only a little rather than having to rehabilitate an existing lawn.

The Right Time

Timing is critical to installing a new lawn into your empty landscape. First, take the time to contact your local building department to ensure you obtain any necessary permits. Then, contact a professional electrician to help you locate and manage any electrical wiring in the yard. Do not assume you can see where all wiring is. It is also necessary to discuss with a plumber were your existing pipes are. Consider all underground utilities in your yard prior to getting started. Underground systems can be difficult to manage, especially when they are older and weakened. Moving substantial quantities of soil around can lead to cracks and damages if you do not take necessary precautions in advance.

The time of the year also matters. Professionals have the skill and experience to lay sod throughout the year in some areas, even in the North. Most nonprofessionals will want to focus on late summer to mid-fall for installing a new lawn. This late summer installation gives the roots enough time to set prior to winter and allows the lawn's roots to develop fully before the onset of the full summer weather the following year. Placing a lawn in the spring will not provide the grass enough time to establish itself before the heat of summer.

Also, take into consideration your time. The first weeks after a lawn is installed will require the most hands-on work for the landscaper. As the lawn matures, it will require less work from you. Plan to install your lawn when you have time to work on it. If starting the lawn from seed, plan two to three months of micromanaging the lawn. If starting from sod, two to three weeks of work is necessary to get the lawn to a beautiful state; however, it takes more intense labor during that time.

Prepping the Soil

Although many people try to avoid this initial step, it is a crucial one. Test the soil. You are making an investment in a new lawn and, therefore, should take the time to learn what the foundation of that lawn will be. A local soil testing service may be the ideal way to get a better idea of what the soil in your yard needs. It will tell you the level of nutrients in the soil, the pH level, and the amount of organic content within the soil itself.

Many people starting a lawn from scratch do so after building a new home. However, residential construction leaves behind some of the worst soil to use when starting a lawn. Further, it is common for residential commercial installers simply to lay down a thin layer of soil to place sod on. Concrete, plaster, and a mix of chemicals may be under that sod.

On the other hand, even if the land is natural and without any debris, it still may not be fertile unless you live in an area known for its agricultural benefits. In both of these situations, take the time to test the soil and to alter it enough to provide your lawn with the strongest start possible.

A good soil base will be at least 6 inches deep, but deeper is better. With this in mind, consider what your area has, what it needs in terms of additional soil, and what nutrients the existing soil has. If you bring in additional soil, test that soil as well because it is not necessarily any better off to start with than what you may have in place.

The best mix for new soil is two parts soil to one part compost material. If you can find a local contractor who offers this type of blend and can assure you the soil is organic, make the purchase. If local retailers do not offer such a blend, mix the soil and compost together yourself using a rototiller. A rototiller is a large device with spinning tines. The tines dig into the top layers of the soil, turning it over and loosening it. The user walks behind the device, similar to using a lawn mower, to turn the soil over, exposing the soil under the top layer.

If you cannot invest in quality soil at this point, it is best to hold off on installing a new lawn until you do. In organic lawn care, it is necessary to establish a strong lawn, with quality soil, that will offer years of beauty to your home. Avoid skimping on how much soil you use, too. Keep in mind that the money you spend investing in an organic lawn started from scratch will come back to you repeatedly in the long term. The lack of needing fertilizers, weed killers, and bug sprays will save you much more than what you put into the soil itself.

Grading the Soil

After you have the right amount of soil, you will need to grade it, or level it. Adding several inches of soil to any yard is a big job. For some larger projects, you will need to invest in a bucket loader or other small bulldozer type of machinery. Another option is to hire a contractor to manage your soil grading and lawn.

To grade the soil properly, spread the soil out evenly. Avoid any large chucks of dirt or divots in the lawn. Work to level the soil out as much as possible. To do this, start at the edge of your home or other building, and pull the soil back away from that location. The biggest concern with grading is ensuring the soil dips away from the building rather than into it. If water pools at the edge of the building because this is the lowest level of the grading, it could damage your foundation.

Grading is an extensive process that requires several treatments of the soil itself. The initial grading process is called a rough grade, and as its name implies, this involves getting the soil to where it approximately should be using additives. During the rough grading process, apply any necessary additives to the soil to get it to the nutrient and pH levels it needs to be.

Additives

Adding nutrients to the soil or changing the pH level in the soil is a necessary step in many situations. What do you need to add? If you have elected to use a compost and soil blend, you have made the most significant of additives already. If after adding that material to the soil, you still find it is not where it should be, consider the following.

If the soil is deficient in nitrogen, based on the results of a soil test, add 1 to 2 pounds of nitrogen to the soil per 1,000 square feet of space. You can use any source of natural nutrients necessary. In this situation, consider using blood meal, which offers a 7 to 15 percent nitrogen increase. In this example, you would need up to 30 pounds of blood meal per 1,000 square feet of space to get the additional 2 pounds needed to reach the ideal nitrogen level. It would increase it by 2.1 to 4.5 pounds per 1,000 pounds depending on the amount of nitrogen the blood meal actually contains.

Chapter 2 provided more instructions on what healthy soil consists of and the levels to work toward to achieve this level of health. Use that as a guide as to what to add to your soil to get it to the levels it should be for optimum health.

By adding these nutrients to the soil during the grading process, the additives are more readily available to the young grass roots as they begin to grow. If you added them later, it would take more time for the roots to have access to the nutrients. It is also more difficult to adjust these additives later in a top dress method rather than placing them right into the soil. The term top dress method means to add the nutrients on the soil, rather than mulching the material into the soil itself. Here, you simply apply the nutrients to the soil.

Also, note that by adding only organic nutrients to the soil as needed, you will not burn any of the grass seed or young plants. Using a chemical-based fertilizer is likely to burn the seeds and young plants in the process.

Grading options

During the rough grading process, it is possible to change the overall layout of the yard. Contouring the lawn with slight hills and waves can offer a more aesthetic look to the lawn. On the other hand, if you plan to enjoy this space with friends and play a few games on it, a more level yard is the route to take.

As you consider your options in your yard's grading, also note the location of structures, including driveways and paths. You do not want to grade the yard to encourage water to drain toward these structures. Further, grading the yard downward into your neighbor's yard is also not a good idea. This could flood their yard, which could lead to problems with your yard later, as well as leading to angry neighbors. Always check with your city to determine if a permit is required for grading such as this.

Aim for a grading of 1 foot or less for every 50 feet of distance, and slope away from your home. By hiring a professional to handle the grading process, you make it far easier to get the grading ideal for your home's unique characteristics. Otherwise, get out the level and work to grade the yard properly with a natural slope if possible.

Final grading

The initial grading gets the soil in about the right place. The final grading allows you to make any additional changes to the lawn you need to and allows you to ensure the soil does not clump. After this grading, you can plant your first grade seed or sod.

Also in this process, you will use tools to help you compact the soil lightly. A drum roller works well for this process, and many home improvement stores now allow home do-it-yourselfers to rent these by the hour. This device features a large, round tumbler that sits on top of the soil. Handles allow the user to push and pull the tumbler. On the side of the tumbler is a hole where the user can add water to the level desired. The user then walks behind the device, pushing it over the soil. Use one filled about a third to a half full with water. By rolling the drum over the soil, you get rid of any air pockets in the soil while also revealing any potential problem areas with density.

You can, and should, go back and make corrections to the final grading as needed to ensure the grading is appropriate after rolling the drum over it. This drum step will also show any rocks or other items in the soil that should not be there. Remove these items from the soil and then rake out the dirt again, adjusting as necessary.

Make one final pass over the yard with the drum roller. This time, compact it less by only filling the drum about a quarter of the way full. This gives the soil some structure to better allow for grass seed and roots to take hold.

Is the soil dry? If it is to the point of being dust-like, saturate the first 1 to 2 inches of soil with water. If the soil is already moist, avoid doing this. You do not want the soil to turn to thick mud; you want it just damp enough to make for the ideal growing medium.

Permanent Edging

Because you are starting your lawn from scratch, it only makes sense to consider permanent edging. Lawns, flowerbeds, and gardens need something to separate them, otherwise they will spread toward each other, creating a nonuniform and difficult-to-manage space. Edging can be a natural and a permanent solution to the problem.

In addition to creating boundaries for the lawn, edging also can save labor. When properly put in place, edging reduces the need for string trimming around these edges. To avoid having to trim, place the edging into the ground so the mower's wheels can run right over the top of it, trimming the edge of the lawn without a trimmer.

Edging can be a major portion of the landscape or it can be a minor element, depending on your budget and design needs. Use brick, stone, or wood for edging. Avoid plastics and other non-natural elements here. It only takes away from the organic look and quality of your lawn.

To edge with bricks or stones, first dig a trench about 12 to 18 inches deep. By preparing this subsurface first, you improve the overall success of the pavers. Backfill with stone dust and compact it every few inches. Then, place pavers or bricks on top, ensuring each one is level with the one next to it.

If you do not plan to use edging around your lawn, you will most likely be pumping toxins into the air as you use an electric or gas-powered trimmer to cut those edges down. The only way to avoid this is to purchase manual trimming tools, which most garden centers offer.

Now that you have the soil down and graded and the edging put in, the next step is to plant grass. Organic grass is, of course, the best route to take.

Selecting Organic Grass

Chapter 3 outlined a variety of grass options. You can select from any of these that perform well in your environment. As you deliberate, focus on a few important aspects. First, ensure the grass you select is an option that works within your area of the country, appearance, desires, and sunlight availability. Take into consideration drought tolerance and the growth rate. Think about the frequency of fertilization required by the variety of grass. You can learn about the fertilization your grass will need by reading recommended planting conditions the product's manufacturer recommends.

Plan to combine three or four cultivars of grass into the grass mixture you select. This is particularly true in the northern states where it is common to grow several types of grass at the same time. By using several varieties, you avoid a nonculture that is more likely to develop disease and produce a more appealing atmosphere for insects.

Which application method to use

Several options are available for starting a lawn. Not all varieties start in the same way, however. Some varieties offer limitations on the available installation methods. Also, take into consideration what options are available to you locally through garden centers or professional landscapers. The main methods of starting grass include using seeds, sprigs, plugs, or sod.

Most people elect to start a lawn using grass seed. It is the least expensive option available, and it gives you the ability to mix various seeds to create the look and feel you enjoy. Using grass seed is labor intensive. It also takes the longest time to fully establish, sometimes more than a year. The only grass not commonly started using this method is St. Augustine grasses,

 which is traditionally installed using sod or sprigging because it is difficult to grow. It requires a longer growth time from start as well. Sod has become a more popular option in recent years, mainly because it has become more readily available through landscapers and home garden centers. This application is the quickest way to reach a full-grown lawn, but it is also the most expensive. In addition, you are limited to grass varieties available in sod in your area. In addition, sod also may not be fully organically grown. If you elect to go this route, ensure you choose only an organically started sod product by asking the distributor.

Sprigging is another option. Sprigs are simply small snippets of grass. It is somewhat like transplanting small vegetable plants into a garden or purchasing pre-grown flowers for your garden.

There is little top growth, but there are substantial roots. Sprigs are readily available in the South and in the West but also are available during the warmer months in the northern United States. Using sprigs of grass is the intermediate option between seeding a lawn and using sod in terms of expense and the amount of time involved. It is more in the middle in terms of costs and for time as well.

Yet another option is plugging. Zoysia lawns, a type of grass, commonly use plugging. Here you have an intermediary between grass sod and sprigs. Plugs are small portions of sod that have a massive set of roots all intertwined together. The plugs are about 3 inches by 3 inches in size, though some are 2 by 3 inches. When placed about 6 inches apart, the plugs grow together in a short amount of time, filling out the lawn. It takes a few weeks for the lawn to fill out, whereas it can take several months for plugs to come in and longer for grass seed. Plugging is more expensive than seeding and sprigging but less expensive than using sod.

Select your grass type based on a variety of factors, especially your budget and your time period for having a fully installed lawn. Determine what is available through your local gardening center as well. Not all options will be available in all areas. If ordering over the Internet, make sure to research the company thoroughly to ensure you get a quality product.

In terms of cost, plan to spend between ten and 20 times as much for sod as you would for seed. Some types of sod are less expensive, such as warm season sod. In addition, the cost of grass seed varies significantly, as does the cost of purchasing straw or using a commercial mulching product to help grass seed grow. For the lowest-costing option but the most labor intensive, use grass seed and then rake the grass seed into the soil and compost. Then, spread a thin layer of compost over the top to keep seeds moist enough to germinate. Seeded lawns require about three times as much watering as sod will. That can also be a factor in selecting the type of grass starter to use.

If you elect to purchase sod, contact a wholesaler directly rather than going to local landscapers, if this is possible in your area. To contact a wholesaler, visit the company's website online and get their contact information yourself. The wholesaler will give you a better price and a better selection of products to select from. Most wholesalers have no problem working directly with the public when the public is purchasing a significant amount of sod, such as to cover your entire yard. Determine if there are any minimum purchase requirements or limitations on where the company will deliver.

Once you have selected a method, install it properly. If using sprigging or plugs, consult the grower's recommendations for installation. This can differ from one company to the next. Sod is simply unrolled into the area you wish to place it. Then, you will firmly pack it down. The grower should provide directions, so be sure to follow them. If not, ask for more information. Those selecting seed should place seed evenly over the lawn area and cover with mulch, compost, and soil or straw.

At the end of this chapter, you will learn more tips for using these methods when installing a new lawn.

Watering After Installation

Once the grass is in place, the next step is to keep the grass growing. Watering is a critical step in this process, but do not overdo it. Watering the lawn too much can be just as problematic as not watering the lawn enough.

Do not allow seed, sod, or sprigs to dry out fully. The soil should not be dry, crumbling, or dust-like. Do not allow the grass to discolor either. These are signs that the plant is drying out. With these application methods, water the lawn frequently but avoid drenching the soil. You only want the first few layers of soil moistened. The surface of the soil needs to remain moist all the time during this initial growing phase.

This initial phase takes some time, especially if the grass is growing from seed. To know when your grass has reached this phase, tug on one of the grass blades. If when tugging upward there is some resistance, you know that the plugs or sprigging are setting. For seed, the initial growing phase lasts until the grass is several inches tall. At this point, cut back on watering the grass to once every two to three days and avoid letting the soil completely dry out.

About six weeks after planting sod, or about the third month after planting seed, reduce the watering to infrequent levels, as you would expect to water a fully grown lawn. Treat the lawn as if it is still a young plant and water as needed.

Maintaining a young lawn

A young lawn is one that will grow unevenly and produce mixed results no matter how you started that lawn. You will likely see some blades of grass grow well, even hitting 6 inches in height within a few weeks. On the other hand, you may find yourself struggling to get some sections to grow even 1 inch. This occurs because you are using different types of grass and simply because not all seeds or plugs will produce the same results.

When it is time to start cutting your lawn, keep the lawn mower's setting at the highest setting for six to eight weeks. Rather than cutting it lower, cut your lawn higher but cut more frequently, as much as twice per week. Sod requires at least a full week of being in place before you can use a lawn mower on it. This time allows the roots to implant into the soil underneath. Most seeded lawns will require about six weeks before you can safely cut it without hurting the individual sprouts, depending on the rate of growth. It is safe to begin cutting after the initial planting stage, when the grass is at least 5 to 6 inches tall.

This initial cutting is critical to the health of the lawn. If the mower is old, invest in a sharpened blade before you run it over the grass. If the blade is dull, it will pull the young plants right out of the soil, destroying the lawn. A lawn mower set too low will damage the plants because it will remove too much and not permit the plant to have enough resources to gather light for photosynthesis to occur.

After a few cuttings, lower the blade of the lawn mower gradually until you reach the desired level. As a rule of thumb, avoid removing more than one-third of the length of the grass blade in any one cutting. Doing more than this damages the plant's chances to survive. As mentioned previously, removing too much of the blade of grass will eliminate the plant's ability to gather energy from sunlight.

As part of the initial process of maintaining a newly established lawn, consider fertilizing the lawn. If you took the time to do a soil test and added any necessary components to the soil, you should not need to add any additional fertilizer to the lawn for at least six weeks.

One nutrient to add is phosphorus-rich material. You do not need to add phosphorus to soil after that initial additive, but adding this nutrient now can help the roots of the grass to establish themselves stronger, leading to a healthier lawn faster. It is particularly important to use this if the roots of your sod are not fully established within three weeks. If you seeded the lawn, the root system should be at least 2 inches deep within three to four weeks. If not, add phosphorus material to the lawn. A good option is bonemeal.

During the first few months of the new lawn's growth, avoid foot traffic on the lawn as much as possible. The more you compress the soil, the more difficult you make it for the root system to grow and expand. If you live in an area where foot traffic is common, try roping off the lawn. Small animals and even pets are normally not a problem, so long as the pets are not large and do not dig into the soil.

Tips for Lawn Installation Methods

For those who are establishing a lawn, the actual method of installing sod, plugs, or sprigging can be challenging. To minimize stress or mistakes, consider the following pointers to establishing your lawn using these methods:

Sod installation

To install sod, grade before starting the process, and then lay out each strip of sod. Using a soft spraying nozzle, soak down each strip with water from the bottom to the top. Then, flip it over and do the other side. Begin fitting each piece of sod into the giant puzzle of your lawn. To do this, start with a strip going straight across the center of your yard. From this point, work outward. Each piece of sod needs to butt up tight with the piece of sod next to it. Continue laying the sod using a checkerboard look. Avoid allowing the strips to start and stop at the same place by alternating with a longer or a shorter strip.

The edges of the sod will shrink inward about 3 percent as the sod dries. By keeping the edges tightly up against each other, but not overlapping, you will minimize any gaps. Any time you need to cut the sod, use a sharp utility knife and be careful because it is easy for the knife to slip on the wet soil. Once all pieces of sod are in place, use a drum roller filled with about a third of water to roll over the sod to help press it into place. If there are cracks, fill them in with soil. Then, water the sod. Avoid allowing soil to erode during the process. If you installed the sod properly, there should be no visible cracks or holes in the finished lawn.

Sprig and plug installation

Sprigging and plugging are common in areas where warm season grasses do well. The process is effective but only when done properly. For beginners, these two methods are the more complex options as compared to seeding and using sod.

First, purchase the right amount of sprigs or plugs. Measure your lawn, and order enough sprigs or plugs to cover your lawn as is recommended by the manufacturer. The company will tell you how much area each package will cover. Plant plugs 6 to 12 inches apart and sprigs 4 inches apart. In both cases, the best way to start is to create a grid using stakes and string. Place each row of string 2 inches from the other string and place each plug or sprig 6 to 12 inches apart within those rows.

As soon as the sprigs or plugs arrive, it is best to plant them. The longer they are without soil, the less likely they are to do well. Have the grid complete before these plants arrive if possible. Use a dowel or bulb planter to create 2-inch holes in each of the locations you will place the plugs or the sprigs. Create a checkerboard look by placing the second row of plugs or sprigs in between the first row's plants.

Next, place the plug or sprig into the hole. Hill up the soil around the base of the blade and cover the roots, but at this point, avoid pushing into place. After you get the entire section complete, use a drum roller right over the top of the plugs. The drum roller should have enough water in it where you can move it, and you are leveling off your yard at the same time. You do not want it so full it makes ruts or too light it is not effective; you need to find the right balance. This firmly pushes them into place, and it will not harm the plants themselves.

Once planted, plugs and sprigs do require attention. You will need to keep the entire area wet at least for the first six weeks. After about six to eight weeks, the grass should have formed together somewhat and should be ready for you to cut it. Lawn plugs will be ready sooner than sprigs. Cut the grass at the highest setting on the lawn mower to allow all of the grass to continue to grow until it has fully come in, and then reduce it.

Realize that sprigging and plugging take time. It can take as long as six to nine months for this type of lawn to come in fully.

Seed installation

For those using seed to start a lawn, you are using the method most commonly used for centuries in planting lawns. The process is relatively successful if done properly and if you give it enough attention after the initial planting is complete.

To start, spread the seed using a spreader. Spreaders are commonly found at home and garden centers. Most spreaders are inexpensive. Set the spreader to release seed at a low rate. Fill the hopper, the container on top that feeds the dispenser, with only about a third of the seed needed for the entire area you plan to plant. For more information on how much seed you need for the area, consult the seed manufacturer because each variety is different. Normally, you will need between 1 to 8 pounds of seed for every 1,000 square feet of soil.

With one-third of the seed in the hopper, walk over the lawn and spread the seed, covering the entire area. Do two more passes each, using another third of the lawn seed for the area on each pass. Make these second and third passes in different directions from the first to ensure even coverage of the area.

Once the seeds are in place, fill a drum roller about one-third of the way full with water, and roll it over the seeded soil. This ensures the seeds are deposited into the soil. It is still necessary to cover the seed because birds and wind can cause seed loss. The least expensive option is to use straw, but straw can be messy and blows away easily. Instead, add a thin layer of organic compost over the seed. This adds nutrients and protects the seed. Avoid using hay because hay will leave behind weed seeds. You can cover with a thin layer of soil, but it may slow the growing process, and you will also not reap the benefits you have from the compost and its nutrients.

Some varieties of seeds, especially those warm season grasses such as zoysia, will need light to germinate. If that is the case with the seeds you have selected, avoid covering the seeds or use a light covering over the seeds. Avoid placing any heavy mulch over lawn seeds at all because the heavy mulches do not allow for proper aeration, which makes it difficult for grasses to grow.

Next, water the seeds down heavily. You may need to water the lawn up to three times per day to help it germinate during the first few days. Do not water so much there is standing water or running water. You want the soil to simply stay moist. Avoid using any type of sprinkler that shoots water out aggressively or at a hard rate.

After about three to four weeks, the lawn will begin to show significant progress. However, it is likely you will find spots that are bare or thin. When this occurs, re-seed the area. If the seeds are poor quality or the lawn does not get enough sunlight, this could lead to a thinning of the grass. Some areas, especially those with limited sunlight, will simply take longer and may require several seedings before coming in successfully.

Hydroseeding?

Another option to consider is hydroseeding. In this application method, water, seed, and some type of mulching material come out of a sprayer and are applied directly to the ground. This method is more expensive initially, but for those who wish to reduce the labor costs associated with seeding or plugging a lawn, this method is effective.

You may wish to consider hiring a professional to hydroseed your lawn. A professional will perform the process in minutes, whereas it may take a novice homeowner several tries to get the process right. You can rent hydrosprayers from some garden centers and home improvement stores. The pulp in the sprayed mixture contains recycled newspapers and phone books with a green dye added. This spray application is faster, and the product used produces a quality layer of seeds. If you do rent one, you will need to purchase grass seed, as well as the proper mulch for the machine. This type of mulch contains paper and wood material in most cases. You will also need to use an agent called tackifier, which works to stick the material to the soil. Many times, you can find this available at retailers that deal with organic large-scale projects for restoring vegetation.

Avoid putting fertilizers into this mixture if you have properly tested your soil and applied the additives your soil needs. If you do use fertilizers when adding seeds, ensure the additives are all organic and not chemical-based.

The application process requires walking around with a tank on your back and a spray nozzle in your hand and spraying a mixture onto the grass, much like watering the lawn with a tank. The mulch product in the hydroseed works the magic here because it offers the seed a bit of nutrient and protection from the elements, and it also keeps the seeds moist during the germination process.

Learn to use the hydrosprayer properly by asking the rental agency questions. You can rent hydrosprayers at lawn and garden centers or other tool rental facilities. However, make sure you are clear about what you are doing. The wrong ratio of water to mulch and seed can lead to problems with the sprayer. It can take some practice to get the entire process right.

In many cases, starting from scratch is the easy way to install an all-organic lawn. You are controlling all of the materials put into place. On the other hand, most people are not willing or able to pull off their entire lawn to follow this process. Instead, they must change what is already in place. In that case, lawn rehabilitation is necessary.

CASE STUDY:
DARIN BROCKELBANK

Darin Brockelbank
Owner of Metro GreenScape
www.metrogreenscape.com

Darin Brockelbank founded Metro GreenScape in 1998. This initially small business helped locals in the Charlotte, North Carolina region to develop well-maintained, healthy lawns.

When asked about the importance of organic lawn care, Brockelbank provides this simple, yet effective view: "This process has been around since the start of civilization. It still goes on naturally in the woods all across the world. As leaves drop from trees and decompose, they form a layer of compost that holds moisture for the plant/tree and also feeds the tree with much needed nutrients. This is also true with lawns; if you get to travel around the country, you will notice rural areas that have not been developed tend to have lawns that look nicer. The reason is during the development of the home, developers scrape off the topsoil these trees have had since the beginning of time, sell the trees as timber, and sell the topsoil to landscapers like myself, leaving the homeowner with no nutrients to work with."

When considering the importance of synthetic fertilizers, Brockelbank compares synthetic products to steroids for people. These synthetics provide immediate, great results, but those results are only temporary. He says, "Organic fertilizer breaks down the soil the developer worked with. Over time, you have layers of dirt breaking down so that the grass roots go deeper to get the nutrients, which makes the turf stronger for droughts, wet years, or any other unusual weather patterns. This process is an investment because it takes years to have a good organic-based lawn — in most cases three to five years — and weeds will come in like never before for the first two years until the turf is strong enough to fight this off."

One of the factors many people are concerned with is time. Getting a great looking lawn can take years, Brockelbank explains. "If a lawn is more than half filled with weeds and has been established for at least three years, it's better to start over. If it doesn't fit those perimeters, then try to work with it."

Chapter 7

REHABILITATING A LAWN

When you consider the benefits of starting a lawn from scratch, you may be thinking about the fact that you can control virtually everything you put into and onto the soil. On the other hand, rehabilitating a lawn already in place is still possible, and in some cases, it can be less expensive and less labor intensive. Before you rip out the old lawn to install a new lawn, consider rehabilitating the lawn.

The first step in rehabilitating your lawn is to understand what its underlying problems are. Why do you want to change it? What is causing the lawn to underperform for you? Oftentimes, the biggest problem is in the way people try to fix the lawn. If you simply try to lay new seeds on top of an already established lawn with poor soil, you are only going to get a poor mixture of results. Your lawn will continue to look poor until you take steps to correct the underlying problems.

Evaluating the Situation

The first step in determining the best route to take for repairing your lawn is to understand what your options are. In short, you need to determine how large your budget is for rehabilitating the lawn and what you are willing to forgo because of a lack of budget and still remain happy with the finished product. The goal is to match your desires with the problems your lawn has and work toward a solution.

One of the first ways to evaluate the soil is to conduct a professional soil test. This process is important no matter how you plan to repair the soil and lawn. In addition to this testing, also dig a hole in the lawn about 6 to 8 inches deep. Look at the quality of the soil itself. The best soil has a thick layer of topsoil at least 6 inches deep. If you have densely packed clay, porous sand, or stones, the soil condition is not ideal for growing a full lawn as it stands. If you lack quality soil, the lawn will always struggle.

If your plan is to add a significant amount of topsoil to your yard, read Chapter 6, and start the lawn from scratch. Otherwise, you can add as much as a full inch of topsoil over the top of your existing lawn to repair the quality of it. If that is your plan, continue with the following steps.

Preparing the Soil

Prior to replanting new grass, it is necessary to repair the soil. To do this, start by mowing the lawn on its lowest setting, as the grass left must be 2 inches or shorter. This will give you the best access to the soil to treat it organically. Once done, you will need to rake up the clippings. If the clippings contain heavy chemical treatment, such as chemical fertilizers, toss these out. Otherwise, compost the material. Do not allow the clippings to remain on the grass.

Next, consider the weeds. If the lawn has a weed problem, meaning that weeds are prevalent throughout the lawn, use an herbal herbicide on the entire lawn. Another option is to purchase a flexible rubber material to place over the top of the entire lawn. You can find this material at most home improvement stores. The texture is somewhat like a yoga mat. This will kill all vegetation in the yard under it, which gives you the ideal place to plant grass. For stubborn or hard-to-remove weeds or grass, simply dig it up. There is no need to be careful about the lawn at this point, especially if you are repairing the entire lawn.

The next step in the process of preparing the soil is to **dethatch** it, which removes all of the dead material from the lawn. **Thatch** is a term used to describe matted grass and nondecaying material that is likely preventing fertilizer from getting to the soil and is offering an ideal place for insects to live. By dethatching, you scratch open the top of the surface of the soil while removing thatch. Once removed, you no longer need to worry about this problem because organic lawns rarely develop thatch. The organic compounds break down these dead materials faster because microorganisms within the soil are active.

There are two ways to remove thatch — either with a mechanical device or with a strong rake. The tines of the machine or the rake will scratch the surface of the soil while bringing up the thatch material. Collect this mass of dead grass, and add it to your compost pile. Perform this process over all of the soil in two directions.

After dethatching the soil, the next step is to aerate it. This process is just as valuable if not more so because it allows air and water to move through the soil better and gives roots the ability to grow. It is best to avoid aeration tools or even spiked devices attached to shoes. These do not help because they do not pull the soil up but rather compress the soil on either side of the hole the spike creates, which does not allow air to circulate any better. Instead, invest in an aeration machine. This machine is available through home improvement rental outlets. Walk behind the machine as it pulls up plugs of dirt and places them on top of your lawn. There will be holes throughout your yard, but that is what you want to see happen. You do not have to remove these plugs from on top of the soil because these plugs will dissolve over time. The only difficulty with an aeration device is these devices are heavy and often hard to use.

Improving Soil Quality

As with any plant, the condition of the soil greatly affects the resulting health of the grass. Soil often needs amending, and once that is complete, the soil can sustain the grass's life longer and with better results. As instructed earlier, obtain a soil test from a professional testing company at this point if you have not already done so. The information from this test will provide you with steps on how to improve the soil so you can create the ideal medium for grass to grow.

When rehabilitating a lawn, improve the soil quality after you have removed debris and thatch from the grass and aerated it. By improving the soil before you put down grass seed or sod, you improve the conditions necessary for those grasses to grow.

Regardless of what the results of your soil test are, it is always a good idea to perform a top dressing of compost. A **top dressing** is simply a thin layer of compost added to the top of your grass. If you are unsure of the composition of your compost or its quality in terms of being good for your lawn, have the compost tested. Most companies that do soil quality testing also offer testing for compost. Most of the time, homemade compost requires adding some nutrients. Macronutrients in particular are necessary, including phosphorus, nitrogen, and potassium.

You may also want to add natural material to improve the levels of magnesium, sulfur, and calcium in the soil. Add organic material, such as fruit and vegetable scraps, coffee grounds, composting leaves and vegetation, and lime. Most types of grasses use these nutrients at a higher level.

Once you determine what type of nutrients your soil needs, add those nutrients into the soil through the compost layer. *See Chapter 4 for a thorough guide to help you determine how to add nutrients to the soil and compost.* Once you have the mixture in place, simply apply a thin layer of the compost material across the top of the lawn already in place or in the patches where you are working to improve the lawn's consistency. The material will naturally enter the soil over the next few days as it rains or as it naturally melds with the existing soil.

Improving the soil quality like this also helps to establish a strong level of fertility for the soil. That means when you go to add grass seed, sod, or other grass to the lawn, those products have a better opportunity to grab hold of the soil and begin to grow.

Replacement Grasses

Now that the soil is primed for growing grass, the next step in the rehabilitation process is to select the types of replacement grasses you will use to fill in those weak spots or to improve the areas of your lawn that need it. The first step is to know what you already have in place. Many people will have some idea of what type of grass they currently have. If you do not, go back to Chapter 3 and look at the descriptions there.

Learning what type of grass you have is critical because some types of grass do not perform well with others. You also want to

take into consideration the color, texture, and overall look the finished lawn will have. Take some time to select the type of grass right for your lawn to fill in bare spots and to thicken the lawn. Even though you may have existing grass, you are likely to need additional seed added to it. Because of the work you will do to improve the lawn's quality, this grass type will likely remain with you for years to come.

Once you know what type of grass you want to put down, the next thing to consider is how to do so. The two main options for rehabilitating a lawn are to use sod or to use grass seed on the bare spots or areas where you have removed significant portions of the dead grass or weeds. You can also use sprigging and plugging in this type of lawn rehabilitation, but it may be best to use this method for rehabilitating smaller areas. In some cases, using plugs or sprigs can be a good option for a larger area, but keep in mind that you may end up with patches of different grass colors and styles if you do not mix enough of the new grass in with the old.

It is difficult to use sod as well. Sod is unlikely to match the existing grass fully. It may look out of place and unnatural. Still, if you can find a good sod mix that works well with the lawn you already have, you can install it here.

Because of the complications with sod, plugs, and sprigs, it is common for people to rehabilitate a lawn using overseeding, which is the process of applying additional grass seed to the lawn's already growing grass. The best route to go with overseeding is to purchase a mixture of grass seed that contains the current grasses in your lawn. You can find a mixture that is the same or close to this already available at your local home and garden center. Ensure the grass seed you select offers only organic material and does not contain any additional chemicals or fertilizers.

In situations where you are unsure of the composition of grass in your yard, take a sample of a few of your grasses to your garden center. Ask the garden center employee to help you identify those grasses and to find organic seed to use. Chances are good that the garden center will have what you need, but if not, you can purchase grass seed over the Internet in a wide range of combinations. Visit Dirt Works (**www.dirtworks.net**) or DFL Organic Seed (**http://dlforganic.com**) for a few options.

Once you have found the right organic combination, you can lay the seed down. It can also be helpful to write down the type of seed blend you are using because most lawns will need to be overseeded at least every other year to maintain the healthy, thick growth.

Planting Grass

With your blend of seeds at hand, the next step in the process is to get the seeds down, the sod planted, or the sprigs and plugs installed. The method to doing this is no different from what you used in Chapter 6, based on the type of grass you are installing into the yard. A few differences may occur.

First, if planting grass seed, it may not be necessary to seed the entire yard. If you are only spot treating the lawn, apply the new grass seed only to the areas that need seeding. You do not have to apply using a spreader either. Simply use your hand to sprinkle the seed evenly over the area.

If you are planting sod, most likely you are planting it in random locations that need help. You do not have to be as specific about the locations or the pattern of laying the sod down. In addition, you can cut the sod into any shape that covers the area and does not interfere with the pre-existing grasses you hope to keep.

One complication that can occur with sod is it can form a distinctive line between the old and the new grass. To avoid this, place the sod down in the most important areas for coverage. Then, purchase a seed mixture the same as that of the sod. Apply these seeds along the edges and outward from the sod into the pre-existing lawn. Doing this will encourage the two types of grasses to blend well and creates less of a drastic line of difference between the two.

If the area you need to repair is large and you plan to plant a significant amount of grass, do so by incorporating the same methods used in Chapter 6 for starting from scratch. Even if you apply grass seed over the entire lawn on top of what is already there, follow the same steps as starting from scratch. The drum roller will not hurt pre-existing grass.

Once you have the grass seed planted, maintaining it is fairly the same as what you would do after laying grass seed or sod over your entire yard. In terms of watering and mowing the lawn, follow the same instructions provided in Chapter 6 as you would for starting the lawn from scratch. You will find that the lawn will likely fill out faster if the existing grass is in relatively good condition.

Make sure to mow the entire lawn at a high level for the first few weeks, even the pre-existing grasses, to ensure the new grasses remain nurtured during those first few weeks of new growth. Within six weeks, you can mow and water as you normally would as recommended by the USDA.

Tips for Successfully Patching the Lawn

Although this chapter has outlined the basics of repairing a lawn, it only offers an overview of the process. Most rehabilitation projects for lawns require patching areas in the lawn that are not performing well rather than rehabilitating the entire lawn. However, it is always a good idea to add a layer of compost to the entire lawn if the soil is lacking several nutrients. This will only add value and health to the lawn in the long term.

In many cases, even the best-maintained lawn will have areas of weakness, even after you have rehabilitated the lawn. This may be a divot or a brown spot. In all of these situations, the best way to fix the underlying problem is patching. Patching does not cover the entire lawn, nor does it cover an extensive area. Rather, use this method to focus on those small areas with significant problems.

Determine if you need to patch

It is not always necessary to patch a lawn. In many southern lawns, for example, within a few weeks to months the lawns will repair the damage left from brown spots or even from dead spots. These lawns tend to have creeping stems known as **stolons** and roots that spread similar to the way rhizomes spread and to the way potatoes will spread, but from a root system as opposed to one single stem. Cool weather grasses, including bluegrass varieties, lawns have this ability as well. The process of allowing the grasses to repair themselves is somewhat challenging, and it takes time.

Should you patch the lawn, then? If you would rather not wait for the lawn to repair itself or if you have a type of lawn that does not spread and repair on its own, patching works well. Many people simply do not want to wait months for the lawn to fill in on its own, so they decide to patch it.

How patching works with seed

In order to use patching, gather a few tools, including a sturdy rake, compost, grass seed, and a hose. The first step is to remove the dead material or the decaying material on top of the soil. You can do this by raking it out. Apply enough pressure to the rake to scratch the top layer of soil, which will remove any dead debris and also open it up better for the grass seed you plan to plant. A bamboo rake is a great choice for this process.

Once you remove the dead material, the next step is to add compost to the area. One of the most common reasons these dead areas occur is disease or a lack of nutrients in the soil. Even if the lack of sunlight leads to the dead spot, adding compost will give the grass seed a better chance of doing well. If you purchase compost, ensure it is all organic or use your own as long as it is fully decomposed.

Once you prep the area, add a layer of seeds to the area. Make sure to put enough seeds based on the seed manufacturer's directions. Once down, add a thin layer of compost on top of the seeds to ensure the seeds receive protection from birds and the seeds remain moist.

Tap down the area with your feet to push the seeds into the ground to give them a good chance at germinating. Over the next few weeks, focus on the patched area. Ensure the soil and compost remain moist but without standing water. Once the grass seed germinates and begins to grow to 3 inches, you can mow the lawn.

Using seed is one of the easiest methods to patching the lawn, but it does take time for the seeds to fill in. It is sometimes necessary to get the job done faster, and for that reason, you may want to patch the lawn using sod.

How patching works with sod

Sod is a good option when you need to repair patches in the lawn quickly. You may need to do this because you are having guests to your home or you may be putting the home on the market and want the lawn to look great. Patching with sod is highly effective but is much more costly than using seed.

In this case, you will need to gather a few materials, such as a straight bladed spade, a utility knife, a trowel, compost, and sod.

Take the time to find the right type of sod to match your yard, especially if you want the yard to look great right from the start.

The first step is to remove the top 2 inches of soil and grass from the dead spot. Never place sod over the top of dead spots because the new grass will not grow well in the area. Instead, dig up the top two layers prior to installing the sod.

Remove all of the affected grass. Shake as much of the soil off the grass as possible to avoid any soil loss in the area. If you remove a significant amount of soil from the patched area, this may cause a dip in the grading of the lawn. To avoid this, ensure enough of the soil remains in the patch area to keep the sod level with the other grass in the area or replace the missing soil with a high-quality variety from the store.

Next, add a layer of compost to the hole created from removing the patch of dead grass. Ideally, you will fill this hole with a mixture of compost and soil. This loose dirt creates an optimal place for the roots of the sod to grow. Loosen the dirt with a trowel and then mix the soil with compost. Even out the layer of dirt in the hole, but avoid compacting it just yet.

Once done, turn your attention to the sod. Using a sharp utility knife, cut a patch of the sod to fit into the hole. Cut from the top of the sod down; then, flip it over and cut from the back to the front of the sod. Avoid pressing down on the sod or tearing the sod with your hands. You do not want to compact the sod at this point. Place the sod into the hole, and fill in the gaps or spaces around the outer edge of the sod patch with compost mixture. Tap down the sod using your feet to make contact between the sod layer and the soil underneath.

This patch area will require a bit more of your time. You will need to keep the sod moist, which may require daily rain or watering. It will take about two to four weeks for the sod to look completely normal and blend in with the rest of the lawn, but it will look better than the brown spot right away.

Rehabbing Your Lawn

It does take some time to rehabilitate the lawn, but doing so allows you to reduce costs and to handle the lawn's problems effectively. Keep in mind that rehabilitating a lawn is possible for many do-it-yourselfers, but you can also call a professional to do the work for you. In either case, with a bit of patience and hard work, the lawn will improve quickly.

CASE STUDY:
JASON COOK

Jason Cook
Savory Sceneries LLC
520-971-2100
www.savorysceneries.com
info@savorysceneries.com

Jason Cook, an expert in creating edible and sustainable landscapes, provided some insight into the process of creating an organic lawn. Cook says, "There are so many wonderful benefits of organic lawn care. The first and most obvious is the lack of harmful chemicals. There have been many studies done that show the negative effects of pesticides on pets, children, and adults from cancer to neurological defects. It also minimizes nutrient runoff because organic fertilizers tend to have lower amounts of nutrients and release those nutrients more slowly. The traditional fertilizers deliver an excess of nutrients that wash away and pollute water ways."

Cook explains that over time, there is less of a need to apply water, fertilizer, and other resources into the lawn because the lawn is healthier.

It has a deeper root system and has a well-balanced microbial community in the soil. The lawn is pest and disease resistant. He says, "Another benefit of an organic lawn is it tends to require less mowing because synthetic fertilizers are like steroids for the lawn. They produce a quick surge of top growth without improving the soil. This means that lawns treated with synthetic fertilizers need to be mowed more often but don't get the benefit of actually improving the overall health of the grass. People tend to think of organic lawns as unable to rival traditionally cared for lawns, but the truth is they often outshine them in the end and last longer with less work over time."

When discussing the difficulty of making this change, Cook says the degree of difficulty a homeowner will experience when switching to an organic system depends on the current condition of the lawn and soil, the climate, the amount of care the lawn received in the past, and the microbial activity in the soil. Cook says, "It can take up to five years to achieve the levels of soil organic matter and microbial activity necessary for proper nutrient cycling. However, I have seen lawns that transition from conventional to organic without a glitch. It is nearly impossible to generalize length of time necessary for conversion as this is highly site specific. Typically, the most difficult part of converting a lawn to organic is getting the soil organic matter to an acceptable level. This is best done with a high-quality compost. Soil testing and observing the lawn are the best ways to determine the current conditions."

Cook says rehabilitating an existing lawn, as opposed to creating a new lawn from scratch, is more cost efficient and easier for the property owner. However, in some cases, replacing the lawn can be the quickest way to the desired results. Cook says it is important to keep a sufficiently dense turf to minimize weeds and improve overall health.

Some people simply wish to hire a professional company to manage their organic lawn care. Is it possible to do this and ensure a beautiful lawn? Cook says before hiring an organic maintenance company, research the company. Review their website, and ask for referrals. "This can help you narrow down who is knowledgeable and professional. Once you have chosen your company, ask questions. What are they doing and why? What products are they using and why? Often, you can quickly see if they are committed to organic products and methods and have experience in this specialized area. Be sure to ask if the company uses 'bridge' or 'transitional' products. The idea is similar to the nicotine patch, letting the lawn off its chemicals slowly rather than going cold turkey. This is really a preference issue and depends on the homeowner's discretion. There are, however, organic options if you want to make an immediate change. I prefer the all organic choice, but the company has to really know what they are doing to keep up the nitrogen level as the soil makes the transition. I typically use blood meal to provide nitrogen and iron to the lawn."

The crux for many is having a beautiful lawn, which organic lawn care does not always provide. When dealing with this question from clients, Cook says, "This question of the luscious lawn comes up a lot. It really refers back to the first question that lists the benefits of organic lawn care. It's possible it may take up to five years to build up your lawn, but in the end, it will be just as full and beautiful as the neighbor's and safer and healthier to boot."

Many may ask, why go with organic? To these questions Cook provides the following explanation, "A lawn can be a highly desirable element in a yard. It cools the air temperature in the yard, provides usable space for recreation, and is simply beautiful and soothing. Add to that the benefits of an organic lawn and you're looking at beauty, function, and health. The choice to have an organic lawn really depends on the person though, whether they're willing to put in the upfront work and really care about the benefits of having a lawn. You can tell when your lawn is healthy and has reached its potential based on observation and soil tests. A lot of people choose not to have lawns in the desert Southwest to conserve water. One of the popular options is gravel instead of lawn to mimic the natural desert look. Others keep their lawns small so they can still enjoy the benefits and keep down the water consumption."

In an effort to share his knowledge, Cook provides more details on composting and preparing an organic landscape.

"Actively aerated compost tea (AACT) is a highly recommended addition to any organic lawn program. It is excellent for increasing the microbial community in the soil, reduces the need for watering, improves the soil structure, and enhances root growth. A surfactant, such as yucca extract, is another good addition to any organic lawn program, especially in the desert Southwest, because it improves the structure of the soil and reduces the need for irrigation.

Regular top dressings of compost are a must because they add organic matter, nutrients, and microbes to the soil. Aerating the lawn is another essential because it ensures a looser soil and allows for deeper root growth. Also, spraying blackstrap molasses — a natural sweetener — on the lawn is a good way to feed the microbial communities in the soil. This encourages the microbes to reproduce and break down the thatch layer."

Chapter 8

TRANSITIONING A LAWN TO ORGANIC

The information in this chapter pertains to the process of weaning an existing lawn off the chemical-based diet it has been on. This chapter focuses specifically on transforming a lawn that depends on chemicals to one supported by the natural, organic processes occurring in the soil. In previous chapters, methods presented helped you get a lawn growing, but now, the focus is keeping it healthy and chemical-free.

These chemicals are as addictive to the grass as sugar is to children. It tastes good, gives them energy, and it provides for an instant boost of improved looks. Nevertheless, the long-term outlook is never good. These initial benefits are fleeting.

To continue the sugar metaphor, the rush chemical fertilizers provide to a lawn is similar to the sugar rush a child feels. The nutrients provided do not last long, which means you will need to add more chemicals to sustain those improvements. Each time you apply chemicals to the lawn, you contaminate the ground water supply and harm the environment as a whole. You also simply sustain the process of needing more fertilizer.

You can avoid this simply by starting the lawn from scratch and using nothing but organic material to provide energy to the lawn. But, most people have a lawn in place and do not want to spend the money to replace the lawn completely with a new one. The rehabilitation process provided in Chapter 7 gave you steps to incorporating new grass into the lawn, but you still need to remove the chemical addiction the lawn struggles with to improve its health. In addition, you may not need to grow new grass in your lawn. You may be happy with the type of grass you already have and its thickness. Nevertheless, you still need to stop using chemical products on the lawn.

This chapter is ideal for those who need to get their lawn off fertilizers and into a healthy place, regardless of whether there is a need to replant grass in the lawn. Use this chapter along with either Chapter 6 or 7 to establish a healthy lawn.

Perhaps the hardest bit of news to take as a property owner is that it will take more than a year to see your lawn go from its chemical-based toxicity to an all-organic lawn, sometimes taking much longer. The longer the lawn has existed on the synthetic chemicals and fertilizers, the longer the transition to organic will take. It will take some time for the lawn to accept nutrients, such as phosphorus, nitrogen, and potassium from natural sources, as compared to obtaining these nutrients from synthetic products.

Transitioning your current chemical- and fertilizer-addicted lawn into a fully organic and self-sustaining lawn is one you should take seriously. By going cold turkey with the chemicals and non-natural additives, your lawn will initially struggle. This is similar to a child going through a sugar withdrawal after his or her parents decided to pull the cookies off the shopping list. It will be difficult for the lawn to perform well at first, but if you fight through that initial phase, the lawn will be better off in the long run.

When your lawn begins its initial synthetic detoxification, you may see dead spots form or the lawn may lose some of its lush green color. The reason behind this is the way natural materials deliver nutrients to the grass differs from the way that synthetic products do. Because there is such a difference in the way the grass feeds, the grass will not receive the nutrients it needs in the manner it is accustomed to in a transition period. Just as the child may slim down and end up with having better energy levels after detoxing from the sugar, the lawn will slowly work toward being healthier, stronger, and overall more of what you want it to be. Transitioning your lawn to an all-organic lawn can be one of the best moves you make because it provides your lawn with the nutrients it needs to last for years to come.

There are two methods to getting the lawn off those chemicals and synthetic products. The first option is to go cold turkey. Simply stop using those products altogether and instead use only organic material to fertilize and feed the lawn. This method ends up giving you an organic lawn faster, but the lawn will take a turn for the worse before it gets better. The second method is to use a bridging method, similar to weaning a person from a medication. At first, you will use a mixture of organic and synthetic products until the concentration of organic materials increases to the point of being the only substance used. This method keeps the lawn green but takes longer to process. Weaning the lawn can take years to complete totally. The cold turkey method immediately stops the process of adding chemicals and, within a full year, the lawn will return to an organic state in most situations.

Although you can elect to take the second option, it is often best to go with the cold turkey method. It will provide your lawn with the fastest way to improve in terms of quality and will quickly cut down on the amount of dangerous pesticides and fertilizers traditional lawn care methods call for.

Preparing for the First Year

The first year of cutting your lawn off from synthetic fertilizers will be the most challenging. The lawn has become dependent on the fertilizers and chemicals rather than turning to the soil for the nutrients it needs. As such, the soil itself has become less alive and depleted of the nutrients it needs to sustain the lawn's life. It is your goal to reinvigorate the soil and lawn with organic material, which is better for the lawn and the soil.

The key is to realize that it will take time. You need to transition to a soil that can go from being nothing more than a method of holding the grass in place to being a life-giving force. During this first year, often called the transition year, you will see the lawn go through various phases.

You will battle every pest and weed in your yard on your own, without the help of any chemicals to do the work for you. That means you will need a trowel, a hose, and herbicide sprays rather than a bug solution or weed killer. The amount of work you put into the lawn during this phase of its life is what will determine what you get out of the lawn. The more time you spend caring for the lawn in this manner, the less time it will take to get from a synthetic lawn to an organic lawn and the better the transition will be.

In addition to being hard work, this process of moving your lawn from a synthetic mess to an organic oasis will cost some money. The amount you spend depends on numerous things, including your ability to get free product to use as organic matter. You may want to talk to local farmers, for example, to get this organic matter. If you need to purchase organic fertilizers, you will spend as much as 50 percent more on these products than you would if you were to purchase synthetic products.

If you feel frustrated at this point, try to focus on the beginning of this book and the benefits of having an organic lawn and garden. It can take time and some money, but the hard work will pay off in the long term. In addition, all of the hard work you put into the lawn now will reward you for years to come. Although you may need to make a significant investment in improving the soil quality this year, it will be worth it because you will not need any type of fertilizer in the future.

Before you transition

Before you begin your transition to organic lawn care, consider the sources of organic material available to you. If you find that your options are sparse, take into consideration your options, the amount you wish to spend, and your desire to have a truly organic and lush lawn. It is also sometimes necessary to test out products before using them on the entire yard. As you will see throughout this book, there are no manufacturer products listed because what works in your area may not work well in another. Rather than offer specific examples of materials that may not be available to you, it is best for you to take the time to find and test your own products on your own yard to see if those products perform the way you want them to.

Consider finding a partner or expert in your area who has the knowledge necessary to answer your questions and to work with you on transitioning your yard to an organic lawn. Sometimes, the questions and concerns that arise are going to be limited in terms of what a book can offer, but a local professional in organic gardening can help. Check organic garden centers or farmers using organic technologies to start. You can find additional help through numerous online sites, too, including GardenWeb (**www.gardenweb.com**) and Organic Gardening® (**www. organicgardening.com**). Both of these websites offer forums where you can ask questions and get advice.

Another source you will want to look for is a company offering organic compost in bulk. You will use a great deal of this product initially, but you will continue to use compost throughout your gardening years. It is, by far, the best amendment product for soil, vegetable gardens, flowering gardens, and shrubs. Many local farms and other distributors may sell bulk compost to individuals. Learn about the options in your area by contacting local farmers' groups and co-ops. Even an online search for local organic suppliers will help produce resources. The more sources you have for compost and expertise, the better your transition year will go. As soon as you start to find options locally, the costs will drop dramatically.

The First Year Plan

The steps you will need to take in the first year are rather extensive, but feel free to elect to do only those tasks you wish to invest your time and money in. To get the full results, follow the plan as closely as possible.

It is important to realize that during this first year, you can make mistakes, forget to do things, or simply elect not to participate in certain steps. You are in charge of your lawn's health and well-being. Because you are not using synthetic products any longer, the overall process is not as rigid. You can have flexibility in the intensity you put into this process.

Initial Evaluation: Springtime

Most people in North America tackle their lawn and garden needs during the spring months. You can decide to transition into a fully organic lawn at any time of the year, but springtime seems to be the best option for most people because it offers a sense of renewed energy. Regardless of when you start this process, focus on those tasks that will offer you the best information and results during the time of year that you use them.

The first step is a soil test. Assuming you are not replacing your lawn as in Chapters 6 and 7, you may not have conducted this test yet. If not, now is the time to do so. This test provides you with the information you need to adjust the soil. It provides a look at the nutrients in the soil and shows you where you are lacking.

In addition to a soil test, also look at the soil by digging a hole about 1 foot deep. Check out what you pull up. It is best to see at least 6 inches of soil, not clay or sand coming out. In situations where you only have a few inches of soil to work with, go back to Chapter 6, and start your lawn over for the best results. It is nearly always necessary to have substantial soil to transition to an organic garden — otherwise the grass will not have enough soil to get the nutrients it needs.

If your lawn looks good and the soil level is acceptable, you can renovate your lawn to add more nutrients to the soil as discussed in Chapter 7. However, if you want to switch to a new organic fertilizer, you can do that, too, and work through these steps.

Another area to focus on is the weed population. The more weeds and types of weeds that are growing in the lawn, the more steps you will need to take to get rid of those weeds. If you do have a significant population of weeds in your lawn, take the steps to get rid of them all before attempting to overseed the lawn. Overseeding will not work if the weeds are taking all of the nutrients from the soil, as most weeds do.

In situations where the lawn is in poor condition and all you do is switch from a synthetic fertilizer to a natural one, the process will be difficult, and it will take longer to work through. It is best to handle any particular soil needs before moving forward in caring for the lawn.

Once you have a solid understanding of what the soil needs, you can treat it. During this first application, follow the steps as described in Chapter 6 for adjusting the soil. In short, you will need to clean up the lawn first, usually using a rake and then a dethatching machine. Once you complete that, the next step is to aerate the lawn. Anytime the soil seems to be compact, it is best to aerate it to remove the debris and dead material from the lawn and open up the soil.

With those steps down, you can begin making repairs to the soil. Do this by adding a thin layer of compost over the lawn. This top dressing of the lawn contains about ½ inch of compost material. This is only the first step. The second step is to apply a compost tea to the soil. At this initial phase, the goal is to give the soil all the nutrients it needs in the best manner possible, so when the grass turns to the soil for its nutrients, those nutrients are easily accessible.

After adding the compost, determine if it is necessary to amend the soil any further based on the results from another soil test. Testing the soil frequently gives you a better indication of what your soil needs at that point. For soils that require more nitrogen, use corn gluten during the springtime for the best results. Corn gluten offers a solution for nitrogen deficiency and also works to prevent weeds. You can prevent some annual weeds and crabgrass from germinating during the spring months by using corn gluten because it makes it difficult for weed seed to grow. Avoid using corn gluten if you plan to overseed the area in the coming weeks because the corn gluten will only stop the seeds from germinating.

At this point, do not expect much from your lawn. This process restores the soil only. The grass itself is unlikely to take a turn for the better, unless it was already dependent on the soil. The amendments made to the soil will provide the ground-work for microorganisms to enter back into the soil. Those microorganisms then work to digest natural fertilizers you added. In this process, the nutrients are broken down so the grass itself can utilize the nutrients. It takes longer for the grass to digest natural products than synthetic products, which are diluted and easily digestible for the plants. However, this natural process will get the lawn greener within a few weeks.

Mowing during initial phase

Many people do not pay enough attention to their mowing habits, and that could be detrimental to your lawn, especially during this transition phase. Spring is the ideal time to inspect your lawn mower for working parts and to have the blades sharpened. It may be time to buy a lawn mower if you have yet to purchase one.

For an organic lawn, especially one undergoing this change, there are a few things to keep in mind. First, select a reel lawn mower if the area is small and easy to manage. If the area is large, purchase a mulching lawn mower instead. In addition, it is necessary to allow all clippings to remain in the lawn rather than removing them. The nutrients from those clippings go back into the soil as the clippings decompose. This natural process is critical to replenishing the lawn.

Another factor with the lawn mower is the height of the blade setting. It is important to remember that with a natural system in place for the lawn, you must select the proper setting for the grass rather than the setting that offers the most aesthetically pleasing look. This means never cutting more than one-third of the height of the grass off at any time. In addition, never trim it lower than 3 inches because any shorter would not allow the grass to have enough surface area to grow. Also, take into consideration any of the limitations or needs of the specific type of grass you purchase. Some grasses need frequent cutting while others do not.

During the spring months, it is likely the soil will remain predominantly moist. When the soil is moist, you can mow a lawn lower and more frequently without any problem. When the soil is dry or when the soil is just starting out, mow at a taller height and mow less frequently.

Getting the mowing process right during this initial springtime change is critical. It will provide you with the best opportunity to transition the grass during the spring months into the harsh summer months.

Focus on water

Springtime offers many considerations for a lawn transitioning to a natural system, and water is one of the key factors. How easy is it to get water throughout your yard? Is there an available water source? More importantly, can your community handle an extensive watering plan? With weather patterns changing so frequently, it has become difficult for some cities to get the required amount of rainfall each year to sustain themselves. If you are not likely to have ready access to the amount of water needed for an optimal lawn, cut back. It is more important to ensure you have a plentiful supply of affordable drinking water than green grass.

In situations where it is possible and economical to water the lawn, there are some rules to follow. First, water the lawn infrequently and only when the soil is dry. Your goal should be to water the grass about one to two times per week. When you do water the lawn, water it heavily so the first few inches of soil are moist. Avoid standing puddles, however. In addition, only water the soil in the morning.

One of the benefits of transitioning a lawn during the spring is the naturally increased rainfall available in most areas. What you will also notice is once you transition the lawn to a natural system rather than a synthetic one, the lawn will need less water overall, allowing you to conserve water in the coming years. This occurs because organic material releases its nutrients slowly over a longer time. This process slows the growth rate of the lawn, which reduces the need for water. In addition, the natural materials in the compost break down over time, which keeps the soil moist throughout that process.

Water is an important factor in this initial phase, but oftentimes homeowners use too much because they believe more is better. Instead, cut back, and listen to the soil and grass. When it is dry, you need to water the soil.

Weeds and controlling them

Weeds are a factor to consider but are often less of a problem than you may think. Weed and feed products that home improvement stores sell manage weeds in synthetic lawns. Once you move to a natural lawn system, you will not use weed killing products, and you will not have any need for them because an organic lawn naturally protects itself against weeds. A thick, lush organic lawn will be a natural weed preventer as there will not be space for the weeds to germinate and grow in the lawn.

Homeowners who have invested in weed and feed products or other weed killers in the last few years likely have controlled weeds effectively up until now. It is unlikely that stopping the use of these synthetic products will lead to a lawn full of weeds. If you do encounter weeds during this transition period, remove them by hand. Unless you have a large problem, such as weeds spreading throughout the lawn, you can avoid using any treatments. If the weeds get out of control, herbal herbicides are an ideal option.

In addition to this, consider the value of tracking weeds. Draw a diagram of the yard, and mark the types of weeds found and the locations of those weeds in your yard. In doing this, you will be able to identify if you have a significant problem and what the cause might be. Often, a soil deficiency leads to weed development. Monitor any weeds growing during the first few months.

Maintaining Your Lawn During Summer

During this transition year, you will need to make changes regarding the way you treat your lawn throughout the year. Summer is no different. These hot months are often the most challenging time of the year for grass because of the intense heat and lack of water. This first summer will be a difficult one for you because you will be tempted to douse the lawn with synthetic products to boost its green color. Avoid doing so.

Unless you have installed a new lawn in spring or gone to extraordinary measures to make changes to the lawn's composition, it is likely the summer will begin to take a toll on the lawn. Even if you added compost and organic fertilizers to the soil, you did not give the soil its huge boost of nitrogen that comes from using synthetic fertilizers. That is fine, so long as you give the lawn some of your attention.

Over the course of the summer, apply compost tea to the lawn. Two or three applications of compost tea will keep the microbes in the soil working, and it will provide you with the best opportunity for a greener lawn. During this initial year, the goal is to build up the microbe numbers in the soil. With the warmth of the weather and the moisture from the compost tea, those microbes will flourish. Give them time to do so.

The summer months mean more struggle for the grass, so take it easy. Raise the lawn mower blade to its highest setting, which allows the grass to get taller and provide more shade for itself.

In situations where water supply is not a problem for your budget or community, keep the soil wet but not to where it pools on the surface. You want the moisture to be as deep as possible. Aim for 6 inches of moisture for the best results.

One of the areas you can make a mistake during this time of year is with organic fertilizers. These organic fertilizers, whether you buy them or make them, can do damage to the grass if added during the high heat because of the high concentration of nutrients. When heated, nutrients can burn grass. Only apply organic fertilizers to the lawn if the lawn has maintained moisture throughout the summer months. If so, a coating of organic fertilizer in the late summer will help give the soil a boost for the coming fall and winter. If the conditions are dry, avoid this. You can apply the organic fertilizer when temperatures come down during the fall months instead.

The summer months do not require a great deal of maintenance, except for mowing the lawn and watering as needed. During this year, you may notice some areas performing better than others. Remember, only treat conditions as necessary, such as removing weeds, because the grass will need time to repair the damage of previous years.

Fall Maintenance and Care

The fall season of the initial year is likely a time when your lawn will begin reacting to the treatments you have provided up to that point. During the fall, grass develops its roots to ensure it can maintain itself throughout the colder winter months. When the fall temperatures decrease, you will notice the lawn needing more care, including more mowing as the grass grows at a faster rate. This is especially true in situations where the climate is moist this time of year.

During the fall months, the growth of the grass may warrant cutting the grass more frequently. Because the temperatures are lower, it is acceptable to lower the lawn mower blade by ½ inch to 1 inch. Do not do this if you are in the process of growing any of the warm season grasses. These grasses are already likely being cut low and should not be cut further. This includes most Bermuda grasses and seashore paspalum grasses.

Another condition to monitor during the fall months is weed growth. In particular, you need to focus on weeds going to seed. If those weed seeds hit the soil, the weeds are likely to be a problem for the coming year. Because you have not used any type of synthetic weed killer, it is likely you will have some weeds develop seeds. Remove them, but be careful. This is another area of lawn care that will initially be hard work. The best way to remove these weeds is by digging them out by hand.

If weeds overtake the lawn and many of them have gone to seed, hand digging is not an option. Instead, use a lawn mower with a bag attachment right over the top of the weeds. Be careful with these clippings because you do not want to reintroduce the seeds to your lawn. You can compost them if you have a hot compost pile in place. If not, consider disposing the seeds in a forested area or in an area where you are not developing the lawn. Weed seed can grow prominently if given the right conditions, but a shaded area is not enough for these seeds to germinate.

Fall is also the time for leaves, and that means your lawn may need more maintenance in terms of raking. But, there are a few things to take into consideration here. First, a good rule of thumb is to leave the grass clean throughout the fall and winter months. This means keeping leaves off the ground as much as possible. Some people like to mulch leaves and leave them on the lawn. This is not a big problem, but if you have a significant amount of leaves, the added material could cause problems for the grass. If the grass cannot get sunlight during the fall because of these leaves, this will lead to disease and an unhealthy winter for the lawn. It is often best to remove leaves either by raking them up or by bagging them with a lawn mower. Add these leaves to your compost pile for use the next year.

Making changes during the fall

Like spring, fall is an ideal time to make any necessary changes to the soil and the grass itself. The weather is favorable, and the timing is right for significant change. Much of North America sees an increase in the amount of rain the area receives during the late August and September months. Because of this increase in rain and the drop in temperatures, many of the biggest lawn renovations should occur during the fall months.

One of the first things to do during the fall months is to give the lawn more nutrition. Spread a thin layer of compost mixture over the top of the lawn. In addition, provide a soaking of compost tea during one of the dry days during the season. In situations where the homeowner has yet to apply any type of nitrogen additive to the soil, now is a good time to do so. In the fall, use approximately 1 pound of nitrogen to 1,000 square feet of lawn, using only organic products.

If you are just starting your change in lawn systems now, follow the spring plan of dethatching the lawn and aerating it now. If you have been following an organic lawn care system since spring and have already dethatched this year, it is unlikely you will need to do so again. If you have noticed a significant amount of thatch as you rake leaves, use a mechanical dethatching device to pull up any decaying material out of the lawn. It is vital that the lawn not have a significant amount of debris in it during the winter months. Debris blocks the sun's rays, reduces oxygen flow, and damages the grass blades.

If you did not aerate the lawn during the spring months, you can do so now. In many ways, the added rain will help the aeration process. You should not need to aerate again if you did so during the spring.

Overseeding during the fall is also ideal. If you overseeded during the spring months, it is unlikely you will need to do so again in the fall. However, if the grass is thin or you did not overseed during the spring, do so now. Those who live in cooler climates should try to overseed during the fall months rather than in the springtime or summer. By seeding now, the new growth will have the ability to get its roots in place before winter and will have nine or more months before it will need to tolerate the heat of summer, which is always difficult on seeds.

Those living in warmer climates will want to overseed warm season grass during the spring months. If you use cool season grass seed, apply this during the fall months instead. Warm season grasses used in the warmer climates will often go dormant during the winter months and may turn brown. But, cool season seeds are ideal for those who wish to maintain a green lawn throughout the year, including in winter.

During the fall months, it is also a good idea to consider if your soil needs limestone. Although many people automatically apply limestone to the grass, this is not always necessary and, in fact, may do more harm than good. Too much limestone can cause the grass to thicken too much or lead to toxic levels for the grass. Before you apply limestone, go back to the soil test to determine if the soil needs it. If so, then apply limestone during the fall months to grass. If not, avoid this step. If you need to apply it, select a high-calcium limestone. This is more nutritious to the organic soil than dolomitic lime because dolomitic lime is high in magnesium and takes away from the amount of calcium being reintroduced into the grass.

The fall plan is more extensive, similar to that of spring. What you do during this season will have a direct impact on what results you will have throughout the winter, spring, and even next summer. During this initial fall season in the transitional year, take care of the lawn, and focus less on what the lawn looks like. Rather, focus on the nutrients needed and the preparation for the upcoming winter months.

Preparing and Maintaining During Winter

Winter can be a dormant time for some lawns, and it can be a time of transition for others. Although you may not think you have anything to do with your lawn during the winter months, you do. This is especially true during this initial transition year from a synthetically grown lawn to an organic lawn.

Most areas of North America see a slow down or near stop in the growth of grass during the winter months. In southern California, southern Florida, and Texas, grass never really stops growing but may slow some. What you do in order to prepare for the winter will matter to the grass's health.

Those living in areas where grass does slow in growth considerably need to mow the lawn one final time before any snowfall. Mow the lawn short, to about a level of 2 inches tall. Doing this prevents snow or ice from pressing grass down into the soil. Because the lawn is more organic at this stage, it can be more attractive to pests, such as mice, if it grows to a high length regularly.

Those living in areas where the grass continues to grow year-round or where you have applied cool season grass seed will want to care for this grass throughout the winter months. You will need to apply nitrogen fertilizer or some type of nitrogen soil amendment in the late fall. This will provide the lawn with the nutrients it needs to remain strong and vibrant through the winter.

Also during winter, in areas where you have overseeded the lawn during the late fall months, it is important to apply potassium-rich fertilizer to the soil to encourage root growth in these newer grass blades. You can find this type of organic fertilizers readily available at most garden centers. The potassium within this fertilizer will provide the grass with much-needed fortification during this time.

During this period of dormancy, it can also be helpful to conduct another soil test, especially if you transitioned to an organic lawn in spring. This will give you an idea of what the soil may need for an upcoming application. It also will tell you how much your soil has improved in the last nine to ten months on an all-natural system.

Most areas will also benefit from an additional application of compost tea in the last weeks of fall, prior to the first frost. This will provide the soil microbes the best opportunity to flourish throughout the upcoming winter, and create the ideal soil conditions for springtime. Until the soil freezes, the microbes will continue to digest nutrients in the soil, which is beneficial even if the grass has stopped growing.

If the late fall has been a dry season for your lawn, apply water to the grass in the month leading up to the first frost. A deep watering can help provide the grass with the water it needs to sustain itself over the winter. This is not necessary if the first 3 inches of soil are still moist or if you have had a rainy fall season. The goal is to ensure the roots have access to as much water as they can handle, so when the freeze sets in, the roots start the winter season nourished.

Winter mistakes to avoid

Once the frost hits, snow sets in, or the cold temperatures stop the lawn from growing, you may feel tempted to mistreat the lawn. You may not realize you are doing so. The frozen lawn and soil is not immune to damage. If you treat the soil during this time of year as pavement, you will damage most of the work you have done thus far this year.

Grass is resilient when frozen, but it will take on damage from walking, driving, or pushing a snow blower over it. If you take a few extra steps to prevent these types of damages, the lawn will look good in the spring, or at least less damaged. The key is pre-winter planning. Take the time to place stakes in the ground at the edges of the lawn, especially in areas, such as curbs, where it is easy to cut the corner too close. Make sure these are high enough and brightly painted to allow you to easily see them against the white snow.

In areas where you have the option of telling the snowplow drivers where to put snow, do so. If the piles of snow get too high, it will take longer for the snow to melt, leading to longer exposure on the grass. That leads to **winterkill**, the process where the poor conditions of winter cause disease and damage to the grass itself.

During the winter months, it can be tempting to use the snow-covered grass as a parking lot for vehicles you may not use. The problem with doing this is it compacts the soil and leads to winterkill. Although you want to avoid others driving on the lawn, it is just as important to minimize your own damage to the lawn by making wise decisions about what encounters the surface of the snow and grass.

Another way you will damage the grass is with the use of chemicals to melt ice and snow. No one likes to get outside in 0-degree weather to shovel snow and ice, but this is preferred over using sodium-based products to melt the snow. In fact, sodium chloride is one of the worst products for the lawn because it is toxic to plants and lawns. Another option is calcium chloride, readily available at most home improvement stores during the winter months and which has the same ability to melt snow and ice. Unlike other products, calcium chloride is organic. It will not harm plants, including grass. For another option, simply put sand down on the ice. Even though sand will not help the ice melt, it will add traction to the snow-covered pathways. Sand has no negative effect on the lawn either.

Perhaps you live in an area where it does not snow, or snows so little there is no extensive problem. In these areas, you may have to deal with heavy rain, which can be just as damaging to the grass as snow is. If you notice any type of soil erosion, you may have a drainage problem in your yard, which needs addressing during the spring. Properly grading the yard will help to avoid this in future years.

The Second Year of Transition

Spring of this second year of transition is likely to be the testing point for your transition into a healthier lawn. Although you committed to switching to an organic lawn care system, this season will test even the most determined homeowners because the spring is likely to bring the onset of weeds. It may take your yard a longer time to green up this year, too, because of the lack of synthetic fertilizers. You may feel tempted to turn toward a inorganic product to get the green to come through. Before you make such a move, realize this is often a sign that your lawn is one step closer to being truly organic.

During this transition year, there will be times of great-looking lawns and times of yellower lawns. This is because of the soil's transition and because the lawn is transforming into a healthier form. The old material, including the toxins, chemicals, and insecticides in the grass and soil, need time to break down. This becomes evident in this second season.

By the time the second spring occurs, the lawn pulls itself away from its chemical dependency. During this time, the lawn is removing toxic chemicals it still contains. Most of these will be broken down in the early portion of the spring. Your lawn is unlikely to green up until after these products are gone from the soil. Keep in mind that as long as toxins, such as weed killers, insecticides, and other chemicals, are in the lawn, the lawn will depend on these substances for nutrients. Once those substances begin to break down and are no longer present, the lawn has lost its immediate source of food. It will not be until the lawn begins to extract nutrients from the soil again that it will strengthen up and become the lush lawn you hope to have.

This second spring is a turning point for your lawn. It is likely the lawn will look a bit worn down, but after an initial application of compost tea, it will begin to green up. You may also notice that this application of compost tea will have faster results than previous versions. This is due to the lack of other fertilizers in the soil now that the toxins are on their way out. The grass is pulling from this compost tea's nutrients more so than it is any other substance.

After you apply compost tea, consider applying corn gluten. This natural nutrient can help keep some of the crabgrass and other types of annual weeds from springing up. If you plan to overseed the lawn this spring, you do not need to apply the corn gluten, but it is best to dethatch the lawn and aerate it prior to applying grass seed. To determine which route to take, simply make a choice. One of the factors that makes organic lawn care so successful is you get to make many of the decisions about what the lawn needs based on the way it looks and, over time, by the way your lawn reacts to the nutrients you provide it.

This second year, you will need to work through the same steps you did during the first year. It is a good idea to have a secondary soil test done at this time — if you have not had one done since the first test. This will give you an indication of what your soil lacks and where it stands in terms of overall health. This soil test should show improvements in the nutrient levels found in your soil, especially if you followed all of the steps during the first year to provide those nutrients.

Once you know your soil's nutrient levels from the soil test, you can then use a top dressing of compost to the lawn to fill in any areas that need additional nutrition. From this year out, it is a good idea to use a top dressing at least one time per year. This top dressing helps provide the lawn with nutrients that the grass removes from it each year.

During the second year, you still need to focus on giving your lawn nutrients through compost tea. The soil is likely unable to completely provide for the grass yet. About once every two weeks, apply compost tea during watering. If you do not have the time or budget for that, at least apply the compost tea once every four weeks.

Another part of the process of maintaining your lawn this year will be managing weeds. The most effective method for reducing weeds is to dig up the initial sprouting and get rid of it. Doing this by hand may be painstaking work, but it will help to keep nutrients in the soil — instead of allowing the weeds to drain your soil's nutrients — and it will help to keep the lawn looking lush and healthy.

As you work through this year's tedious steps of caring for the lawn, remember that you are just one year away from having a healthy lawn. If you are transitioning to an organic farm instead of just a lawn, it takes a full three years of following this process to get the organic certification. At this point, you will be only one year away from that point. If you plan to grow crops for sale as organic food, check with your local chapter of the USDA to learn the specific steps for improving the soil in your area. You can also request information on how to receive this certification. For the purpose of this book, just realize you are close to having an organic lawn.

After the Second Year

After working through this transition process for two years, you will feel more confident in your ability to know what your lawn needs. You may notice it is not as green as it should be, and that might mean the lawn needs another application of compost tea. By year three, you will feel more confident in your abilities to manage your lawn over the long term.

Two years after you first began the switch over to organic lawn care, you should see a lawn greener than or at least as green as it was when you applied chemical products to it. It should green up faster this year than it did in past springs. Greening up faster simply means the lawn will go from its dull, almost yellow color to a vibrant green more quickly. Most of these lawns have become strong enough now to fight off weeds, so you may see fewer leafy intruders.

At this point in your lawn care routine, you will need to take care of your lawn as you see fit, based on the lawn's particular needs. If you do not feel confident in your ability to do this, hiring a contractor to do the work for you is a possibility. However, if you have followed everything in this book thus far, you have the skills and know-how to keep the lawn looking strong and healthy for years to come.

Each lawn is somewhat different in its needs. You can opt to obtain a soil test each year to determine what the lawn does or does not need, but you should be able to back off getting soil tests done as frequently. Unless you notice a problem or believe there could be a problem with your lawn, it may not be necessary to get another soil test for two or three years.

Do take steps at this point to keep the lawn's health in the front of your mind. Monitor its performance throughout each of the seasons. Dethatching and aerating are two tasks you will still want to do yearly during the springtime. Once the lawn becomes strong, it will become more independent. Microorganisms found in the soil will begin to eat away at the thatch material and will deposit plenty of nutrients while also creating pockets of air under the soil. The lawn will self-aerate and dethatch itself over time.

One of the other benefits of the lawn this year and likely for years to come is you will need to mow less frequently. Less frequently may mean mowing once every two weeks instead of weekly, but this depends on the type of grass, the rainfall in your area, and other factors.

Taking care of your lawn still requires a bit of hands-on work each year. Apply compost tea to the lawn at least a few times per year, more if you believe the soil needs it. You will know your lawn needs compost if it shows signs of yellowing or less green coloring to the grass. In addition to this, most lawns will benefit from an application of corn gluten each spring because this product contains an ideal source of nitrogen. It will provide nutrition the grass needs and will help with weed control. You could also apply calcium to the soil each year, but if a soil test indicates a high level of calcium in the soil, avoid applying any of this nutrient to your lawn.

At this point, you have the ability to step back and let your lawn do well on its own, aside from the basic maintenance tasks. In many cases, those who have put a lot of hard work into maintaining their lawn are less willing to decrease the lawn maintenance tasks. Many people want to remain a bit more in control of their lawn and will spend more time managing the lawn's care. However, it is better to allow nature to work as nature does and let the lawn become the self-sufficient ecosystem that it can be.

You Can Bridge the Lawn, But Beware

In this book, you have learned the method to transitioning a lawn using a cold turkey method. Some people, though, cannot manage to see their lawn looking anything less than perfect year after year. For those who want to maintain a green lawn and want to bridge to organic lawn care more slowly, you can do this with a combination of synthetic and organic blends.

It is healthier for the lawn to avoid applying any additional synthetic chemicals because this only extends the length of time it takes to transition to a healthy, organic lawn. However, manufacturers do produce chemicals that mix both organic material and synthetic products.

To know the difference in these products, read labels carefully. Under the U.S. Organic Marketing Law under the USDA, any product the manufacturer labels as organic must be made of natural plants, minerals, or animals. To get around this, some companies label products as organic-based, which does not mean the same thing. These products may or may not contain organic material, but they nearly always contain at least some types of inorganic material in them.

Although more research is necessary to provide a clear understanding of these effects, it is possible that adding synthetic products to organic material can lead to the organic material becoming less helpful to the lawn. The problem is these synthetic products are toxic and can cause harm to the microorganisms living in the organic matter. This often means you are doing little to benefit the soil with these products. Although organic-based products are less expensive than true organic products, it may be better to spend more money on true organic products that offer better results.

Should you bridge the lawn, instead of going cold turkey, by using these blends? Although the decision is always up to the homeowner, it is not likely to be the best move for any lawn. As mentioned, the first year of transitioning a lawn to a fully organic lawn will be difficult on the lawn's appearance and usually on the homeowner, too. This method of transitioning, however, is the best route to take to get to the goal of a truly organic lawn.

CASE STUDY: MARK BORST

Mark Borst
Borst Landscape and Design
260 W. Crescent Avenue
Allendale, NJ 07401
(201) 785-9400.
www.borstlandscape.com

Mark Borst, owner of Borst Landscape and Design, provides some excellent viewpoints and tips for today's organic lawn care owner.

"Organic lawn care is a system that requires patience. The goal of the entire process is to get organic material applied and absorbed into the soil, which in turn balances the soil, retards/repels pests, and allows for substantial growth and turf health. The benefits of an organic program are reduced amounts of chemical pesticides and herbicides being used, limiting those applications to treat only severe issues."

The difficulties of transforming a lawn become quite worrisome for some. Borst says it is not as simple as abstaining from using chemicals. He says because organic programs do not offer immediate satisfaction in the form of a newly installed lawn, homeowners will need patience to yield results. When converting a lawn to an organics program, the rehabilitation will depend on the lawn's weed and pest infestation. "If the infestation is not too severe, an organic process will be successful over a period of time, but if the lawn needs a radical change, starting from scratch may be more beneficial."

Asked about why he started his business, Borst says, "We became very aware of a void in environmentally safe procedures and products in our marketplace back in 1995. We took the initiative to become a pioneer in this field and offer our clients, many with children and pets, a safer alternative to the traditional chemical lawn care treatments.

A lawn is an aesthetically pleasing asset to your home. The benefits of producing oxygen, controlling erosion, and creating a great area for outdoor activities is well worth the effort, time, and expense. You'll know it was worth it when you look outside your window and look at the best of nature right in your own yard."

Chapter 9

WATER AND THE NATURAL LAWN

*W*ater seems like such a simple element. Although every living thing needs water, many people do not put much focus into water itself when caring for the lawn. As you convert the lawn to a natural lawn, water becomes an important part of the process, and it will greatly determine the outcome of the finished lawn.

Step back to science classes you may have had in high school. You may remember that water is one of the three necessary nutrients plants need to flourish. These plants require sunlight, carbon dioxide, and water to complete the photosynthesis process. This process helps the plants to grow and remain healthy. Each blade of grass is its own plant, a small system that demands all three levels of nutrients to maintain its health and to thrive.

Water is a critical element to grass for several reasons. Water is vital to create the photosynthesis process. It comes in to the grass from the roots and rises to the tip of the grass blade. In doing so, it maintains temperature of the plant and helps it to breathe. This process, known as transpiration, is what happens inside the plant. Outside the blade of grass, water is also a necessary tool. Here, it works as a way to transport nutrients to the plant while also working to flush away toxins. Rain moves the soil to the roots of the plant so the roots consistently have a strong source of nutrients.

In many parts of the United States, water is readily available. Lawns may not require a great deal of supplemental water simply because the rain is plentiful. In these circumstances, water is not something most people think about frequently. When rain is scarce, the health of the grass is at risk. Water is not as abundant as it used to be in many areas of the United States. Because of the changing climate, there are more areas of the country, and of the world, that are without the rain needed to maintain the needs of animals and people, not to mention grass. On the other hand, some areas of the country get an incredible amount of rain. In that case, too much rain can damage crops and leave people at risk of flooding because too much water allows the soil to remain vulnerable to disease.

In each of these situations, the plants in these landscapes need to adapt to that rainfall amount, whether it is not enough, just the right amount, or too much. The key here is to determine how to manage your rainfall levels effectively. In this chapter, the focus is not only on how natural lawns need water, but it is also on how to conserve water and how to use it wisely so as not to waste one of the world's most precious and limited resources.

Various Factors Affect Watering Needs

As you work through this chapter, keep in mind your local conditions. Even in areas near your home, the rainfall amounts will change drastically year after year. It is up to you to adjust the way you use water and the way it integrates into lawn care. An interesting fact is that in terms of a lawn's health, a lawn that gets less water and remains dry is healthier than a lawn that is over-watered. This is a commonly misunderstood aspect of lawn care, and it could affect the look and feel of your grass.

In addition, keep in mind that your lawn's needs will change as it transitions to a healthy, organic lawn. At this point in the book, you may have worked through the process in total. In that case, your organic lawn is likely to require far less water, sometimes half as much, than it did when you started the process. If you are still applying synthetic fertilizers and other toxins to the lawn, the lawn needs more water because of the increase in the rate of growth these synthetic products cause.

One of the worst culprits of this demand for increased water is pesticides. When you apply these products to the grass, you will need to water them deep into the lawn to ensure the toxins reach the area of the lawn where the pests lurk. This is not good for the lawn or the microorganisms that can keep your lawn healthy over the long term because the toxins kill off the beneficial microbes in the soil. This is another example of why it is best to stop using pesticides and instead rely on a healthy, organic lawn.

Maintaining a healthy lawn

For those who are making the transition into a healthy, organic lawn, water plays an important part of that process.

The timing makes a difference

Timing is one factor that affects your lawn's water use. Many people water their lawns whenever they have the time to do so. But, the ideal time to water a lawn is in the middle of the night and early morning. Between the early morning hours of midnight and 9 a.m. is best, though it is probably the most inconvenient for most people.

When you water the lawn during this time, the water is given the time it needs to enter into the soil during these early morning hours. When the sun comes up, it will gradually warm the soil, and the water will evaporate. This helps the soil to dry out over the day. When the evening comes around, the soil is relatively dry and less likely to develop fungus. If you water the grass in the evening, the water remains there for an extended amount of time without any way for the excessive amounts to dry, which promotes the growth of fungus.

Some people prefer to water the lawn during the day because of the convenience of the timing. However, when the sun is shining and the temperatures are higher, never water the grass. This is perhaps the worst time to do so because the sun will simply evaporate the water before the plants can absorb it. As a result, the plants dry out quickly because they do not have access to the moisture they need.

The amount of water affects health

The second factor that plays an important role in the health of the lawn is the amount of water used. As mentioned previously, too much water is worse for a lawn than not adding enough water. With that in mind, consider how much you should water.

In general, the goal is to water a lawn so it gets about 1 inch of water per week. Although this is a good guideline to follow, it is just a basic answer to the question of how much water. Each lawn's needs are different. The more time you spend caring for your lawn, the more you will learn about what it takes to maintain a healthy lawn in your area. Your lawn is unique because of its landscape outline, the type of plants you own, and the overall composition of the soil. You have to become an expert on how much water your lawn needs.

If that sounds a bit daunting, especially if you are a first time lawn enthusiast, it does not have to be. The first step is to understand the factors that play a role in this equation. Five primary elements play a role in how much water the lawn needs: the soil type, natural rainfall levels, sunlight, the type of grass, and the evaporation and transpiration process.

To take a closer look, consider the type of soil you have. If the soil is sandy, it is likely you will need more water for your lawn than if you have a clay-based soil. The difference here has to do with the overall ability of the soil to hold on to moisture. Those homeowners who do have this sandy soil structure can improve the soil's ability to retain moisture by simply adding organic material to the soil.

Another factor is the type of grass you have. Some grass types require more watering than others. For example, if you have a Buffalo grass or a centipede grass, you will need less water than those who have a bluegrass variety. If you do not know what type of grass you have and what its watering needs are, visit the U.S. Department of Agriculture's website for Natural Resources Conservation Service at **http://npdc.usda.gov**. Search for the type of grass you have to learn more about this grass's particular needs.

One factor you cannot control is the amount of rainfall your area receives each year. The amount of rainfall affects the amount of watering you must do to maintain the lawn's health. It is also important to understand the rate at which the soil and plants lose water through evaporation and transpiration. Sunlight is another area you cannot control. To learn more about these rates in your area, visit the National Climatic Data Center online at **www.ncdc. noaa.gov**. There, you can see the published rates of rainfall in your area, as well as the evapotranspiration rates. What you will notice from doing a bit of research at the site is that the amount of rainfall and the amount of available water changes throughout the country fairly regularly.

Because this rate of rainfall does change so frequently, it becomes necessary to consider your lawn's needs as they change. It is possible to stay on top of this change by simply paying closer attention to the amount of rainfall you get. You can purchase a rainfall gauge — sold at any garden center — to document the amount of rain your lawn actually gets. You can also use a sprinkler that measures the amount of output. If you decide to forgo buying a rain gauge, you could also just use a jar placed in the yard to monitor rainfall.

Each of these elements plays a role in lawn care. The more sunlight the grass gets, for example, the faster water evaporates. This increases the evaporation and transpiration process, which affects the water level in the soil. What do you do with this information? Use it to help you to determine when you need to water more or less. This will provide you with a basic guide to follow, but it is not as important as monitoring the condition of the grass and of the soil itself. Take the time to look at the soil to notice any signs of dehydration. When you probe the soil, it should be wet to a level of at least 4 inches. If this does not occur, you need to water the lawn more.

The grass will also tell you when it needs more water. Look for the leaf blades to fold into each other when the grass needs more water, for example. Another sign that the grass needs more water is if you notice footprints in the grass. The grass should spring up within a few minutes after you step on it. The color of the grass can also be an indication. Thirsty grass will go from a green color to a blue-gray color before turning a brown color.

One more factor to consider about the amount of water is that not all areas of your lawn need the same amount of water. Those portions at the base of a hillside, for example, need less than the grass at the top. Areas where the drainage is less than ideal may need less water, and shaded areas will need less than those areas in full sun. In this case, it is necessary to take a closer look at your lawn to determine the areas that may need more or less watering.

How often you water your lawn plays a role

Another important aspect of watering your organic lawn is how frequently you water. A better word for this is infrequency. When watering a lawn, the goal is to saturate the soil enough and then to allow the grass to benefit from that water for as long as possible. This is important for water conservation and for the health of the lawn. Rather than watering it by a set schedule, notice when the grass actually needs water.

How can you ensure the soil remains wet if you are not watering it all the time? Instead of watering frequently, water infrequently. When you do water, water deeply. Continue to water the lawn as long as the soil absorbs the water.

Watch the movement of water as it hits the surface of the grass. If you notice that the soil absorbs the water easily, the lawn is thirsty and needs a good soaking. However, you do not want to see puddles form. Look around for signs that the water is moving away, such as water flowing down the driveway or into another area of the garden. This is a signal that the soil is wet enough. The benefit of watering the soil and grass like this is that it encourages the plant to develop deeper roots. When water is available deeper, the roots must grow and stretch deeper into the soil. This provides the grass with more stability and helps it to grow stronger as a result. The roots not only get stronger, but the soil at the surface can also dry out slowly, which keeps fungus and other diseases from developing in the grass. If you follow this rule, the grass will have deep roots, which can withstand droughts better, too.

Alternatively, if you were to water the soil frequently but only in small amounts, the water would remain at the top of the surface. This causes the roots to remain shallow, and the roots often lack the strength necessary to keep the grass upright. Another problem that can occur is deeply watering the soil too often. Deeply watering the soil is the goal, but do this infrequently. Watering deeply too frequently keeps too much water in the soil. This is often noticeable in grass that sloshes when you step on it.

If this has led you to confusion as to when to water, remember a few key rules. First, the look and feel of the grass is the most important sign. You want to ensure the grass needs water before you apply it.

Another step you can take to learn if the grass needs water is to follow a few guidelines, specifically for the growing season. If you live in a region that has rainfall 25 inches or more per year on average, your goal is to water the lawn deeply just one time per week. If you live in an area that has less average annual rainfall, water two times per week in this manner. Keep in mind the amount of rain you get also plays a role in this process. When it rains enough to keep the soil moist at least 4 inches below ground, you do not need to water.

More factors to keep in mind

A few additional factors play a role in when to water the lawn and how much water to use. Specifically, take into consideration the mowing height used, the amount of fertilizing you do, and the amount of wind you receive. Each of these three elements matter but to a less significant level than the other factors mentioned thus far in this chapter.

First, consider your mowing height. Mowing height does play a role in the amount of water the lawn needs. If you are in a drought spell or you want to water less, mow the lawn at a higher level. If you enjoy lower-cut lawns, you will need to water more frequently to maintain the soil's moisture properly. This difference occurs because of the amount of shade that taller grass yields. The shade taller grass offers helps to slow the evaporation process. In addition, if you mow the lawn more frequently to keep it shorter, the grass must work harder to regrow the top portion of the grass blades. As a direct result of this, the lawn needs more water to maintain that growing process.

Next, consider the amount of fertilizing you do. Using synthetic fertilizers will lead to more watering. Grass that uses this type of fertilizer needs more water to maintain the energy to grow. This is also true of those fertilizers that are organic. Although organic fertilizer products do not force the need for as much water as synthetic products, they still require more water than unfertilized grass because of the way in which fertilizers affect the grass. Fertilizers encourage the grass to grow and to develop fully. Because you add the fertilizer, the grass will want to grow faster, which leads to the need for more water. Take a closer look at the ingredients that make up your fertilizer. If it has a high level of nitrogen, it will encourage the grass to grow at a fast rate and require a higher amount of water. Whenever there is a dry spell or instances when the rainfall levels are lower, avoid using any type of nitrogen-based or nitrogen-heavy type of fertilizer. This will cause the grass to dry out the soil even faster.

The final element that affects watering for maintenance is the wind. You cannot control the wind, but it does play a role to some level in the amount of watering you will need to do. Consider your hair, for a moment. After taking a shower, your hair is wet. If you are in no rush, you may let it air dry, which may take a while to fully dry out. On the other hand, if you are in a hurry, you take the blow dryer to your hair to speed up the process. The same process occurs with grass. If there is wind, the soil will dry out faster than if there is no wind. If there is wind and hot air, this will speed the process of drying out the soil even more. For those who live in an area with significant wind on a regular basis, installing windbreaks, such as taller shrubs and trees, can reduce the amount of watering your lawn needs because it will help prevent water loss.

Allowing the lawn to go dormant

During times of drought, or when there is less rain, it is natural to allow the lawn to dry out and to turn brown. It may not look appealing, but it is a cycle of natural earth sciences. If you do this, will you lose the lawn and have to start over? What you may not know is that most lawns have a mechanism within them that helps the lawn to go into a period of dormancy. Dormancy is the lawn's natural way of dealing with droughts. This can help you decrease the amount of watering you need to do in an instance where there is not enough water supply to do so.

Most lawns will have the ability to enter into and maintain a state of dormancy for four to eight weeks. This is a type of automatic survival mechanism for the lawns. When there is a situation where the amount of water is minimal, this mechanism stops the grass from growing. It helps the grass preserve its energy during this time. When rainfall improves, or when the lawn begins to receive water again, the lawn will green up within a few days to a week. This is not to say the grass will always come back. If it is a prolonged drought beyond the length of time the grass can maintain the dormancy state, the grass will die. It is rare for this to happen in areas that receive 25 inches of rain annually because of the depth of water in most of these soils.

For those who live in other areas of the country, it is necessary to determine what you wish to do during periods of dormancy. If water levels in your local area are not at risk, you have the choice to maintain your lawn by watering it regularly to ensure it remains green. On the other hand, when the lack of rain is significant and has lead to conservation of water for human consumption, do not water your lawn.

In some circumstances, people will make the decision to allow the natural rainfall that occurs to be all the water they apply to their lawn in that they will allow the grass to slightly brown and enter into dormancy whenever there is not enough rainfall.

This is acceptable as long as you realize you are taking a slight risk that the lawn will die. If the lawn does die, you will need to replace it. This is an instance where you will need to make this decision based on your own needs, desires, and budget.

As an extra layer of protection for those who do allow the lawn to enter a period of dormancy because of a lack of rainfall, apply just a ¼ inch of water to the lawn every two weeks. This will keep the plant just wet enough to remain healthy. Do not give it more than this if you plan to allow the grass to remain in the dormancy period though. Doing so will wake up the grass, which may lead it to grow and begin to use energy much too quickly.

Also, note that some types of lawns, especially those found in southern states, enter this period of dormancy each year during the winter months. In this instance, the period of dormancy does not arise from a lack of water but rather from the cold weather during the winter months. These grasses enter into the dormant period for the same reason — to conserve energy. If the lawn enters into this dormancy, it will brown over. In the spring months, the grass will quickly green to allow the growing period to resume.

The Quality of Your Water

The quality of the water you feed the lawn is as important as anything else you add to the soil. Depending on where you live, the water quality may range from hard water to soft water and from chemical-filled water to well water. The quality of water and the amount of water available are important factors to take into consideration when you water your lawn. If you live in an area where you have a well, monitoring the level of water available is important. During drought years, you may not want, or cannot afford, to water the lawn when the well's level is dipping too low. Even those who live in a city need to remain conscious of the level of water available. City water often comes from lakes, rivers, or aquifers of water that lie deep under the ground. Your city may instruct you not to consume extra water or may put limitations on how much or how frequently you can water your lawn.

Water quality ranges widely throughout the world. In most cases, city water goes through a purification system. If you use well water, the water coming into the home has no purification but still goes through a cleansing process within your home's water system to remove impurities. A softener system helps cleanse the water, for example. Your home may have hard water or soft water. It may have chemicals, such as chlorine and fluoride, added to it from the local water treatment plant. Alternatively, your water may not have any of these. In all of these situations, what is in the water affects the way your lawn will grow when it receives water.

Do you have hard water or soft?

One of the first things to keep in mind is the difference between hard water and soft water. Do you know what you have? If you have hard water, you likely have water that does not soap up in the kitchen sink or water that leaves a ring around the sink's edges. Those who draw water from a well often have hard water. This water makes it difficult to clean with because the soaps cannot activate properly to allow it to do so.

It is possible to treat hard water. To do so, most people must add water softener to the water. This allows the water to become more useful and better to drink. But, lawns are different in that lawns will perform better with untreated hard water. Hard water contains higher levels of calcium and magnesium, both important elements to a plant's growth and development. By using hard water, your plants are likely to perform better, and that includes lawns.

When water contains softeners, it also gets an added layer of sodium. Soft water has a higher sodium level, which can lead to severe health effects for the lawn. You can tell that a lawn has too much sodium from its water supply if the lawn yellows. In some situations, too much sodium can actually cause the soil's overall composition to degrade. With poor soil and too much sodium content, plants, including grasses, can die.

Many people who have water softeners in their homes will likely pull out the garden hose attached to the homes' water supplies to water the lawn. As a direct result, they will apply softened water to the lawns. It is not convenient, nor economical in most cases, to have a source of hard water outdoors just for the lawn. You can overcome this obstacle, though. The best way to overcome the sodium-rich softened water is to use it sparingly, or at least less often than you currently use it, especially if you have noticed any signs of yellowing on the grass. If the grass needs water, use stored rainwater. You can place large containers in your yard to collect rainwater. Then, apply the collected rainwater to the grass whenever possible.

Another solution to dealing with softened water is to build up the soil's quality. Adding compost to your lawn a few times per year will build up the soil's overall composition and will improve water drainage. If water can drain properly away from the grass, this will reduce the likelihood that sodium will build up in the soil. The sodium still enters the soil, but the drainage washes away the excess.

What about city water?

Those who live in a city may draw water from a municipal supply. That water is purified often numerous times over to ensure it is a healthy option for people. On the other hand, you may be using a well instead. The water in the well may contain a variety of substances. Unlike a city water system, you may not know what is in the well water. Wells can contain fairly clean water, depending on whatever rainwater and ground water is available in your area.

What is in your water? In either of these situations, it is a good idea to try to learn what is in the water. You can obtain a water test through your local water supplier, or for those who use a well, you can turn to a third-party provider to come to your home and to test the water. If you are unsure about your water's composition, testing it is really the only way to learn more about it. Water testing, like soil testing, is not done at home. Suppliers can test water from municipal systems for you and may test water for wells in your area. Determine if the local water company offers testing. Visit this website to find a list of companies offering test of water supplies: **http://water.epa.gov/scitech/drinkingwater/labcert/index.cfm**.

Keep in mind that most municipal water supplies do contain two ingredients you should learn about: fluoride and chlorine. The supplier adds fluoride to help to prevent tooth decay. Adding fluoride to water began in the 1960s and continues today. Poor dental health is present in most industrialized countries, so the World Health Organization encouraged countries to add fluoride to water. The U.S. government also took steps to do this. Water treatment plants add chlorine, the other substance in municipal water supplies, to cleanse and disinfect the water. This chemical does help clean the water, but too much of it can be risky for human health and for the health of your plants. Water suppliers monitor the level of chlorine to ensure safe levels for human consumption.

Like sodium, too much chlorine in the water you use on your grass will lead to problems. Chlorine is a natural chemical and is one of the nutrients plants need to grow and remain healthy, but it is the amount of chlorine that can damage your lawn. In its natural form, chlorine in ground water and soil is in small amounts. When you apply treated water to your grass, you put far more chlorine on the grass than is considered a normal level.

For those who believe chlorine could be a problem or for those who wish to eliminate the problem, fill a container with water, and place it in your yard. Allow it to sit overnight before applying it to the grass. Do this each time you plan to water the lawn. By allowing the water to sit out overnight or longer, the chlorine will evaporate. This keeps high chlorine levels at bay and protects the lawn.

Although you do have to monitor the chlorine levels in your water supply, fluoride remains one of the biggest factors you will need to deal with when it comes to caring for your lawn. The excess fluoride present in your municipal water supply will accumulate specifically in the tips of the grass blades. With a high level of fluoride present, the end result is that the grass plants are more likely to burn. You may notice this by the tips of the grass blades turning yellow. This is **necrosis**.

If you suspect this is a problem, you will need to take steps to improve the situation. To do this, focus on raising the pH level of the grass to 7. In many cases, you can do this by adding lime or a wood ash to the soil. By adding these natural elements to the soil, the pH level of the soil will rise to 7, which is neutral. When that occurs, the fluoride found in the soil will convert to a form that is not accessible to the soil any longer. This will prevent the grass from absorbing the fluoride and, thus, will treat this problem effectively.

Should You Invest in A Filter System?

For those who are concerned about the minerals and other additives found in the water they apply to the soil, one solution to overcome this is to use a filter system. The filter system ties into the water access point, such as the outdoor spigot. Much like a filter system added to your indoor faucet, these filters help to remove many of the impurities from the water and remove mineral deposits. Some types of filter systems can remove fluoride effectively. Not all remove the same material though. If you do purchase one of these systems, make sure to learn about the specific types of material removed from the water to ensure it removes those chemicals and elements dangerous to the lawn.

The drawback to using these filter systems is the cost. Installing this system is a one-time payment, but it can be expensive. Depending on the extensiveness of these systems, it may cost more to maintain the system as well. Because these devices use filters, you will need to replace these filters as necessary as well. All of these factors add up to a high cost for the homeowner. This type of system is often best for those looking for a highly effective product and treatment option for their soil. If you are looking for a way to guarantee and control the water supply to the highest level, using these outdoor water filtration systems can be worthwhile to you. For others, taking the steps mentioned thus far, without water filtration, can be an effective way of dealing with mineral levels in the water.

Other Water Options and Concerns

There are many areas of the country focusing on finding new solutions to handle water shortages or better irrigation methods. For the at-home gardener, your lawn may be important to you, and as such, you may be looking for a few new ways to get the water you need and to disperse it properly.

For those looking for an innovative way to handle their water needs and concerns, consider the following examples. Each situation is unique. You may need to manage the excessive water you receive while others are looking for ways to water their lawn inexpensively. In all circumstances, the homeowner must find a solution that works for his or her particular needs.

Harvesting rain

One of the ways many people manage water needs is to use a technique called rainwater harvesting. This process captures rainwater and allows homeowners to reuse it on their lawns. This particular method has been helpful in areas of the country known for droughts. In areas where droughts are common, such as in the southeast portion of the United States, it has become important for locals to find ways to reduce using water from rivers and lakes and instead to depend on other methods to fill gardening requirements.

To begin harvesting rainwater, all you need is a rain barrel. The larger the barrel, the better, but choose a barrel right for your needs. You can use these barrels in various ways, but perhaps the most effective method is to use them to collect water from downspouts, which are those areas on your gutters where the water falls over the edges and normally drains onto the ground or into a sewer system. But, you can use this rainwater, which normally is the healthiest option for lawns. By collecting it in these large barrels, you can then store it and use it during drier conditions. This method allows you to make better use of rain.

Depending on your needs, you may wish to use one barrel under each of the downspouts on the roof, normally at each of the four corners of the building. Once the water drains into this area, you can easily siphon it off using buckets or a hose. How much water do you need? For those who wish to apply 1 inch of water to their lawn of 1,000 square feet, estimate that you will need to have more than 600 gallons of water collected. For those who wish to apply that amount to an acre of land, you will need to have more than 27,000 gallons per acre of grass. Keep in mind you can also use this water for other needs, such as for watering gardens and other plants in your landscaping.

To take this to the next level, consider investing in an underground water storage tank. This is a large tank placed under the ground. Water flows from openings throughout the landscape and into the containment device. Because of the installation cost associated with this tank, this is a significant investment. It is recommended for those who have an extensive need and wish to manage water consumption to the highest level. These systems have pumps to make the water easily accessible, much like an outdoor faucet works. After these containers' initial installation, though, the costs of watering your lawn or caring for other water needs are virtually nothing.

Gray water

Gray water is a term used to describe the type of water you have used for something in the recent past. This is a method of collecting water similar to harvesting rainwater, but instead of rain, you harvest the water from other uses. You can harvest water from the laundry you do, from bathtubs, and even from bathroom sinks. This water is safe to use for watering a lawn, and you can use it for most of your plant's watering needs. The only place you do not want to use gray water is on gardens that will produce edible substances — this is not an option for a vegetable garden because of the soap residue, for example.

What about the residual chemicals in this water? For the purpose of collecting this water for use on the lawn, it is acceptable to use. In most cases, the amount of detergent or soap found within gray water is low in comparison to the amount of water present. Nonetheless, for those who wish to have a completely organic landscape — with no chemical compounds at all — using gray water may not be an acceptable option. The only option is to ensure that all harvested water comes from only organic-based sources, such as from sinks where you only use organic detergents.

Gray water is not black water. **Black water** is the water that comes from sewers, kitchen sinks, and dishwashers. This type of water has too much of a risk of having bacteria and other toxins in it, so it should not be used in your lawn care needs. It contains pathogens and viruses that require proper filtration and treatment before the water can be useful again.

Using gray water is a method many people are considering for watering lawns, but to use it, you have to find the right method for collecting this water. Collecting gray water is difficult for most people because of the way these systems drain in your home. Imagine carrying a large bucket of water from your laundry tub up the stairs and outside to the lawn, and then dispersing that water over the lawn. This is difficult to do at best. In addition to this, some local ordinances may ban people from using gray water in this manner because of potential contaminants from those who may mix black water with gray water. Before you consider it, contact the local code enforcement agency, such as your local city hall, in your area and see if there are any particular bans or limitations on gray water usage — these limitations are different from bans on black water usage.

If you can use this method, start by using the water coming out of your washing machine. This appliance often drains through a hose. By funneling that hose — any type will work — into a collection container, you can collect this water easily. Depending on the size of your washing machine, you may see 30 to 60 gallons of water coming from your laundry. Once a system is in place for your washing machine, consider collecting from bathtubs. Using this method, you may end up resorting to bailing the water out of the bathtub and putting it into a water collection container outdoors. This also works with siphoning using a hose. In both cases, it is somewhat cumbersome depending on where that bathtub is located and where your water collection container is located.

For those who wish to take this level of water usage and conservation to the next level, consider installing a plumbing system in your home that allows you to collect gray water throughout the home. Specifically, you will need to design a system that allows you to collect water from specific sinks and appliances that are safe to use and funnels the water into a collection bin placed outdoors or wherever you plan to use it. It is also possible to have these systems drain into an underground water storage tank such as the one described earlier for collecting rainwater. This is another aspect to discuss with a local code enforcement officer before you begin to use this method.

If you do begin to use gray water on your lawn or on other plants, monitor the overall health of your lawn. Observe any type of damage, such as any color differences in the lawn. In some households, using detergents and bleaches can make gray water less desirable to use on lawns or plants. You may not be able to know if the level of detergents or soaps in your gray water is safe until after you begin to use it. If you notice any curls on the tips of the grass blades or any yellowing on the plant, discontinue using the gray water, as it could contribute to disease in the grass itself. It is a good idea to test the gray water on a specific, small area of the yard before you use it on the entire lawn. Experiment with it for a few weeks prior to making a decision.

Wetting agents

Wetting agents are helpful in some areas. **Wetting agents** are topical additives to the soil that are especially useful in situations where the soil needs specific aid to absorb — and keep — water. They are compounds that help the soil absorb water more readily. To do this, wetting agents release the tension in the surface layer of the soil. This tension is what prevents beading and paddling from forming.

To know whether this solution can work effectively for you, consider what the soil in your area is like. Soil can be absorbent or it can repel water, depending on the type of soil you have and various other conditions. In most areas, the top layer of the soil is resistant to accepting water because it is under the constant strain of the sun. The sun's rays dry out the soil, and dry soil has a harder time holding on to liquid. Imagine dry soil as dust compared to the absorbance of wet soil like a sponge. As such, it is likely this soil will be limited in the way it can conserve water to keep the grass wet. Wetting agents can help in these situations.

If you live in a dry area or if you experience a dry spell, a wetting agent can help reduce the amount of watering your lawn needs by up to 60 percent.

You need to keep in mind a few things about wetting agents. First, using a wetting agent does not mean the grass does not need water; it just reduces the amount of water you need to apply to your lawn by capturing water that would otherwise run off. In addition to this, you will need to continue applying natural fertilizers and composts to your lawn as recommended. This wetting agent also does not take the place of those nutrient-producing organic materials.

Another concern for those using this product as a wetting agent is for those who have compacted soil or heavy clay soils. Because of these materials, the water cannot drain into the deeper soil levels, and therefore, the wetting agent is not as effective. For those who wish to make the investment in wetting agents for their lawn, be careful about the application. If there has been a drought or a lack of normal rain levels, apply the wetting agents as soon as you notice any level of stress on the lawn from a lack of water. Look specifically for when the lawn begins to turn brown. This is the best time to apply them. You will need to water the lawn after applying the wetting agent or wait for the rainfall to occur to get the most benefit from using them.

Keep in mind that you can also use wetting agents when establishing a new lawn because they help keep the lawn seed from drying out. Although they add to the cost of establishing a lawn, in climates without regular rainfall, these agents can be highly effective at reducing the amount of watering you need to do.

When purchasing wetting agents, specifically look for a granular or a liquid form, and choose the method best for your particular needs. Remember that you are building an organic lawn, and using synthetic wetting agents is not acceptable under an organic lawn care regiment. Instead, make sure this product is all natural to ensure your lawn benefits from its use. You can find wetting agents at most garden centers or consider buying online at sites such as Greentrees Hydroponics (**www.hydroponics.net**).

When applying a wetting agent, the directions will tell you the best application method. Test the product in a small area if you have not used it previously. This ensures that if the product does not work, you have not lost your entire lawn to the process.

Warning about soaps

In some circles, there is discussion about using various dishwashing soaps as a way of creating a wetting agent for the lawn. Although, it may or may not be effective, this method is not recommended. Using any type of dishwashing or other soaps in the lawn can stress grass that is damaged from the heat or from drought. It also works against the concept of an organic lawn. Instead of using these products, turn to others that are all natural.

About Watering

When it comes to managing your lawn, there is no doubt that watering is an important part of that process. It is also important to note that you should water within your limitations and needs. Over-watering is never helpful. In situations where water is minimally available, it is often necessary to focus on using creative measures such as those discussed here to help ensure your success.

Perhaps the most important factor to remember when it comes to watering a lawn is the lawn should be the single most important factor in determining watering needs. If the lawn's soil remains moist to a depth of 4 inches, you do not need to water. If the grass is not wet enough, apply just enough to get it wet to that depth, but no more. You do not want a super-saturated turf because this allows disease to develop at a faster rate.

You can get as specific and as detailed about your watering needs as you would like. In many cases, you can get creative about the ways you can water your lawn, such as saving water from rainfall in buckets. On the other hand, in drier spells, you can simply allow the natural processes to occur for the grass to enter a dormant stage. Getting to know your grass is the key factor in having success with managing watering needs.

CASE STUDY:
ADRIENNE STAUFFER

Adrienne Stauffer, owner
GreenerGreenGrass
24 3rd Street
Peaks Island, ME 04108
Adrienne@greenergreengrass.com
www.greenergreengrass.com
888-688-2469

Adrienne Stauffer is the owner of GreenerGreenGrass, a company that sells liquid organic lawn care products. The company sells many of the products found throughout this book, including organic fertilizers, soil aerators, and soil conditioners.

When asked about the advantages and disadvantages of an organic lawn, Stauffer replies that the benefits include having healthier soil, which naturally promotes healthier grass. Noting the disadvantages, Stauffer says, "Some perceived disadvantages of organic lawn management may include more time required to maintain the lawn — this actually decreases over time, as an organic lawn will sustain itself and require less maintenance — as well as the presence of some weeds. There are no truly effective organic herbicides, and hand pulling is required, but a healthy organic lawn will naturally crowd weeds out as the grass plants become stronger than the weeds." She also notes that this type of lawn care can be expensive initially, but in the long term, organic lawns are more affordable.

Stauffer also discusses the obstacles involved with moving from a conventional lawn to an organic lawn. "Conventional lawns depend on chemicals, which make the soil 'dead' by eradicating the good bacteria and other organisms that live in it," she says. "The first step in transitioning to an organic lawn is rehabilitating the soil; if this is not done properly, the grass plants won't have the nutrients they need to live. Compost is a great way to return bacteria and nutrients to the soil."

One of the benefits of talking to Stauffer is the expertise she has in organic lawn care products. She offers some interesting information about these products, which are safe for children, pets, and for the grass itself. She states, "In 2011, we will also be introducing a herbicide enhancer that allows customers to use 50 percent less weed killer."

It can be difficult to determine which products are best for your soil and your particular needs. To this, Stauffer adds, "Our Soil Booster blend is an excellent first step for switching from conventional to organic lawn care. Not only does it add beneficial bacteria and microbes to the soil and restore the balance of soil life, it will also help to remove synthetic chemicals from the soil more quickly. Aerator Blend is a liquid soil aerator that works by pushing soil colloids apart on a microscopic level, which creates space for air, water, and nutrients to reach the plant roots."

What about pests? A healthy lawn can often lead to a larger number of pests. When asked how to manage them, Stauffer says, "Insect pests can be repelled with a garlic spray. Other pungent sprays with cloves and thyme can also work. These treatments do not actually kill bugs, but they repel them and keep them away for up to a month after treatment. Weeds are best handled by pulling — yes, it is a lot of work, but the effects are long lasting. They can also be spot treated with a natural herbicide such as vinegar, but be careful not to spray the grass you want to keep."

She concludes with a bit of advice about expectations on switching to an organic lawn. "Have realistic expectations about the way your lawn will look and the work required. Organic lawns usually have a few weeds and should have multiple (native) grass types, so it may not look as uniform as you expect."

Chapter 10

GETTING CONTROL OF WEEDS AND PESTS

What are weeds? What you define as a weed may in fact not be a weed. These plants are loosely defined as any type of plant that tries to grow in the lawn without the gardener welcoming them. Weeds are not always negative, and in the grand scheme of things, it has only been since the late 1940s that most Americans have taken to creating lawns and landscapes devoid of all outside plant life.

Since that time, there has been no limit to the amount of products and methods used to reduce these intrusive plants from entering the lawns. Preventing weeds from growing in a healthy lawn is a challenge. After all, what plant would not enjoy this rich soil with healthy reserves of nutrients? At this point in the organic lawn care program, you are a natural gardening pro now. You can take steps to limit weeds or allow them to grow freely because you realize they are a natural part of the lawn. For those who want to take the least invasive approach to managing weeds, simply mowing over them along with the rest of the grass is a satisfactory solution. For others, the need to dive in and find a way to get rid of every weed that dares to creep in is the bigger focus.

According to *Weeds and What They Tell*, a book written in the 1950s on weeds, there are some 1,175 plants classified as weeds today. The book, written by Ehrenfried E. Pfeiffer, is an important source of information on understanding weeds in the natural lawn. It is recommended for anyone who plans to incorporate a strategy for getting rid of every weed that enters, or tries to enter, the landscape. You may come out understanding why weeds are valuable to the health of your grass. To further explain this, consider the material covered in this chapter.

Understanding Weeds and Reacting to Them

There are several steps to go through to understand what weeds are and what to do about them. The first step is to relax because weeds are a normal element of most lawns. Before that bottle of weed killer draws you in, take a second to think about your new option — you do not need to handle weeds as extensively as you might have done before you installed a natural lawn.

Another way to look at weeds is to consider what they do for the lawn itself. Even with several varieties of grass, the lawn cannot sustain itself. You need to add compost material to the soil to give it the nutrients it needs to maintain the plants growing there. When there are some weeds in the mix, those weeds provide a source of nutrients for the soil and later for the grass itself. Not all weeds offer these benefits, but varieties, such as white clovers and bird's foot trefoil, can benefit your lawn in the long run. In these cases, just mowing the weeds is all you need to do to turn that weed into something beneficial for your lawn itself.

Does this mean you should allow weeds to overtake your lawn? The answer is no, but you should carefully assess the situation before you dive in to weed care. How many weed varieties do you have? Are the weeds a more significant aspect of the lawn's makeup than the grass itself? In situations like this, you need to control the weeds but not necessarily eradicate them.

Identifying weeds

Once you understand how bad the problem is, you can identify the weeds present in your lawn so you can then determine the appropriate action for the weed. Invest in the previously listed book by Pfeifferor or use Michigan State University's online resource at **www.msuturfweeds.net**. It will provide you with the identification steps necessary to pinpoint the specific variety. This book will limit the focus on distinguishing if the weed is a type of unwanted grass or an unwanted broad leaf plant, such as dandelion. Other leaf varieties include chickweed and ground ivy. Unwanted grasses include crabgrass and Bermuda grasses.

As you consider the varieties of weeds, learn if the weed is an annual, perennial, or a biennial. This helps you determine the right method for controlling the weed. Annual weeds will generate from seeds and will grow to produce flowers that produce new seeds. By cutting their life short and removing them prior to the plant reaching that germination stage, you can stop these seeds from forming. The best way to manage these weeds is to not allow the weed to produce any seed. For those weeds that are biennials, they will come back for a second year — they have a two-year life span. As with annuals, you can cut the number and severity of biennials by getting rid of them before the plants create new seed. This will reduce the amount of weeds in your lawn overall.

For those plants that are perennials, your weed-killing approach is a bit different. These plants germinate from seed, but they will also continue to populate with runners that spread underground. These not only grow flowers that seed, but they also create **rhizomes** — horizontally growing stems found underground — and will create stolons to help them to survive. **Stolons** are branches growing above ground. These weeds will make it through the winter if you allow them to. They will need an effective treatment to get rid of them, which means digging up the weed from the roots and removing it from the lawn. Even when you do this, you may find these weeds coming back — it can be difficult to remove all of the underground rhizomes that will allow the plants to continue to grow. In this situation, you may need to change the soil conditions to make it less hospitable to the weeds trying to inhabit it.

Before moving on, take into consideration the steps you have taken this far to create a natural lawn. You have created an ideal climate for grass and other plants to grow. You have selected a healthy seed variety, and you have taken the time to treat the soil itself to ensure it provides the ideal conditions for plants. If you have taken these steps and the others listed in this book, chances are good you have created a healthy lawn that is less likely to have serious weed problems than the synthetic lawn you originally had.

With that thought in mind, remember that you do not have to spend a great deal of time and money learning about weeds. You can actually apply basic information in this book and have a full-looking, beautiful lawn resistant to disease and weeds. You may never have to know what type of weed you are dealing with, though you can of course research and develop an action plan for dealing with those weeds as it fits your particular goals.

Understand what the weeds mean

For those who have a weed problem they want to improve, the next step is to understand why the weed is present in the lawn. The key to organic weed control is fully understanding what is causing the weeds and tackling that underlying problem rather than just removing the weed from your lawn. No matter how many weeds you pull up or spray with herbicides, chances are good they will come back repeatedly until you learn what causes them to appear.

Weeds are much the same as any other plant, including your grass. In order to do well in the soil, they need the right conditions to be present. The key factors for weed growth are the same as for grasses: the right combination of a balanced pH, soil life — such as microorganisms — the right amount of organic matter present, and the right moisture level to do well. Of course, these needs are different for your lawn than they are for weeds.

One way of looking at weeds is as an indicator to tell you what could be wrong with your lawn. If weeds are present, the lawn's needs may lack in some way. The weeds provide you with information you should respond to for the lawn's sake.

Consider the various ways you can improve the soil. For example, you may do everything you can to prevent weeds but for some reason, you notice crabgrass growing. Crabgrass, a type of weed, is likely to grow near the driveway and near sidewalks. Even when you try to dig it up and remove it, the crabgrass is still present. What is the reasoning behind this? This area of your lawn likely gets more foot traffic than other areas. As a result, these areas are more compacted, and therefore, the grass finds it harder to grow here, but the crabgrass grows well in these conditions.

If you do not take the time to fix this problem of crabgrass in this area, it will continue to come back repeatedly. The crabgrass will grow because it needs only shallow dirt amounts to grow well. In this particular situation, all you need to do is aerate the lawn properly to loosen up the dirt — and perhaps encourage foot traffic to remain on the pathway instead.

For the most common types of weeds, there are solutions. For example, if you notice you have a large amount of dandelions in the soil, this indicates the soil is too rich in nitrogen. If you have a large number of clover plants growing in the grass, this could mean you have too little nitrogen. Knowing these facts is helpful, but it is not information you must have to treat the weeds. For practical use, you may want to try a few other tips to help you remove these weeds from your soil.

Saying Goodbye to Weeds

Many people do not care where the weeds came from or why they are there; they just want a way to get those weeds out of the lawn for good. Perhaps the key to creating this type of turf is to simply do so and not worry about the weeds. If you have a thick, lush lawn, it is unlikely that weeds will grow there because the grass blocks the weeds from growing. In order to get your lawn to this level, some may resort to using chemicals. This is not something encouraged here because it goes against everything taught this far.

Instead of using chemical products, it is best to turn to other methods to get rid of weeds. The good news is you have several options to use to accomplish this goal, and each of them is safe to use on an all-natural lawn.

Totally wiping out those weeds

Depending on where you are in the lawn-creation process, it may be possible to completely kill off all plants in the grass in the hopes to getting rid of weeds. If you have already invested in a whole new lawn, you should not have a significant number of weeds. This option is best for those who have mostly weeds in their lawn and little grass.

Another solution to consider is one mentioned earlier in this book — purchasing a flexible type of black rubber from a home improvement store and spreading it over the top of the area where the weeds are growing. This process is called **solarization**. It works by allowing the sun's heat to bake the weeds enough to kill them. This method is also safe to use. Any type of product you place on the grass in an effort to cover up the grass and weeds, such as using newspapers instead of black rubber, should be organically acceptable to the lawn. With that in mind, you can use other products in this way.

If you decide to take this route, go back to Chapter 6 and work through the steps to create a new lawn from scratch. Make sure to test the soil to determine what nutrients it lacks and to supplement naturally as needed to ensure weeds do not grow back.

Spot treating weeds

In lawns that are well established and have just a few areas where weeds are sprouting up, it may be necessary to spot treat those areas. If one or two weeds are present, this does not mean you have a significant problem, but it means that weed seed got into the lawn. This is especially the case if this is the first instance of the weeds showing up in this location.

If a few single weeds become present, dig them out using a spade. This process really takes only a few minutes to accomplish. Take note of what type of weed it is, and make sure to remove the entire root of the plant to keep it from growing back.

What should you do if an area of the lawn has a large number of weeds? Instead of digging the weeds up individually, use the vinegar and citrus oil method for that small area. Then, replant grass seed in the area after the weeds are gone. This option is best for those who have a specific area where too many weeds are present to dig them out.

Pre-emergent

Another option for you to consider is **pre-emergent control**, which is a method that allows you to get more control over the weeds by stopping them from going to seed. Numerous companies sell products that can help you accomplish this, but avoid them. Many of these products, even when marketed as semi-organic products, contain unwanted chemicals. There is another solution for those wanting to use an organic system.

The best solution is to use a product that is a corn gluten treatment. This product is effective at treating weeds prior to their emergence, but in order to see success, you must apply the product at the right time; you will need to use corn gluten on the grass two to three weeks before you expect the weeds to germinate. Research the type of weed you expect to occur to learn when this will happen. Apply the corn gluten at any time during the year, but you will need to know when weeds are most likely to germinate in your area. This can make the process more difficult to use because this will change from one area to the next.

Keep in mind that applying corn gluten will stop all seeds from germinating. Do not apply it to the lawn in the six weeks prior to applying any grass seed to the lawn. This solution does not get rid of weeds already in place. It is also a strong source of nitrogen. If your soil already has a high percentage of nitrogen in it, this may lead to too much nitrogen in your grass. Perform a soil test to ensure you will not have too much nitrogen in your lawn.

Modify your soil

As mentioned previously, good soil health will minimize the amount of weeds that grow. If you have problems with weeds, the conditions just are not right for the soil at this point. Focus on your soil for weed control. Use the resources provided throughout this book to guide you in creating a healthy soil content for your lawn. The soil test is the foundation of this because it will provide you with information about what is wrong with your lawn so you can easily find solutions to overcoming the underlying problem.

One particular type of nutrient you should ensure is present in your soil is calcium. Calcium is an important nutrient for soil, and without it, weeds will appear. If your soil test indicates that the soil lacks this particular nutrient, applying calcium will provide you with the best possible treatment of the weed population. Apply calcium throughout the year to prevent a deficiency.

Mowing as a weed treatment?

The way you mow your lawn could be part of your problem with controlling weeds. You will find more information on proper mowing techniques in Chapter 12, but for right now, just know mowing your lawn properly will cut down on the weeds.

Although it is not recommended to do so often, when lawns are beginning to show signs of weeds, mow with the bag attachment. Normally, there is no benefit to mowing with a bag attachment because you are removing the ends of the grass that could turn into fertilizer for the growing grass after it decomposes. However, in order to get as many of those weed seeds under control, bag it. The bagging lawn mower will help pull up all of those seeds, including those hard to manage dandelion seeds. Then, dispose of these clippings. Do not apply them to your lawn again because this will only provide a place for the weed seeds to grow.

These methods of removing weeds are all natural. They work with your lawn's care and can provide you with the safest method to get rid of the weeds without actually using the synthetic chemicals that can kill your good intentions of creating an organic lawn.

Although getting rid of weeds is important, it is also important to know what else lurks in the grass seeds. Specifically, insects could be wreaking havoc on your lawn just as those weeds are.

Pests in the Lawn

Pests could be an important indicator of health in your lawn. In fact, pests can often be good for lawns. Throughout this book, you have learned about developing a soil that attracts and builds a complex microorganism center in the lawn to boost the overall health of the lawn. Still, people want to find a way to get rid of the most annoying of creatures lurking in the lawn: insects.

In most cases, the insects in your lawn help improve the overall composition of the lawn. They dig and create holes that aerate the soil and, by doing so, give the roots of your plants room to grow. Pests help break down the compost and other materials added to the lawn so the plants have access to the nutrients. Even when these insects die, their bodies decompose, creating a rich nutrient level for the soil.

There are times, though, when the level of insects in the lawn gets to an unhealthy level. This is the only time you should try to reduce the population of pests in your lawn. What is the solution for getting rid of all of these pests? It is not to head out and to purchase substances created with harmful chemicals to spray on your otherwise natural lawn. Even organic varieties of these substances simply are not safe to use nor are they necessary. Instead of these techniques, focus on a cultural solution. A **cultural solution** means finding a way to treat the underlying pest problem using a method that is safe and similar to some of the steps you took to protect your lawn from weeds. In other words, you will take a good look at what is happening in the soil that allows these pests to become a problem while also using steps above ground to minimize their presence. This process will help you get rid of pest problems for good without relying on any type of product.

If you do have to reach for a spray to target these pests, make sure it is something that will do only minimal damage to the soil, the plants surrounding it, and the other organisms in the lawn that are necessary. You will find some products that are all natural can accomplish this, but you do want to ensure the products you use are going to be highly effective so you do not continue to use them. Before doing that, though, it is highly recommended to consider any of the methods listed here to get control of the pests using a natural method.

Naturally control pests

Four methods are available to help you gain control of your pests and lawn diseases using natural solutions. These methods include cultural change, physical controls, biological controls, and botanical controls.

The cultural control applications can be one of the best options available. This method involves using soil amendments, applying natural fertilizers, and mowing the lawn properly. Using this method, you want to use natural changes to the structure of the lawn to help you see changes in the pest-control levels. For example, if you take some steps to improve the quality of the lawn or to change the way you care for the lawn, you create a culture where the lawn is not as ideal for the pests. You can change the mower blade or rake the leaves up and dethatch the lawn. Take steps to limit the amount of water the lawn gets. These changes will force a change in the pests and often will help you get rid of them.

In addition, consider planting disease-resistant cultivars as a control method. Try a new grass variety for the lawn that is more disease and pest resistant, such as Kentucky bluegrass or Aurora. These hybrids are better able to prevent pests because they contain a fungi, such as endophytes, that helps strengthen the grass.

Incorporating these changes into your landscape is most likely to give you improvements. In many cases, these improvements are enough to settle the pest problem to a satisfactory goal.

Making physical controls

This particular type of pest control means applying some physical action to the pests yourself. The goal here is to take steps to get rid of the pests physically. One option is to dig up the area affected by the pests and to remove them Then, remove the soil affected, including the brown or yellow grass, and replace the lawn with new seeding. You can apply sod to this area instead.

For some pests, specifically leafhoppers, webworm moths, and chinch bugs, one of the simplest solutions is to get a shop vacuum. Suck up the bugs and transplant them somewhere else. As simple as that sounds, it works because these bugs are on the surface of the grass and soil and are removed easily.

Another way to make a physical change to the area to control pests is to regulate the amount of sun the area gets. These pests may do well because of the available sun or because of the shade. If this is the case, adding shade or removing shade in the area will make a difference in the overall control of pests.

Biological controls

When it comes to biological controls, think about the natural enemies of the pests and incorporate them into the landscape itself. This is a simple solution, but takes a bit of know-how about the type of pests you are dealing with and the environment they need to be healthy. One of the ways you have already done this is by incorporating compost into the soil. When you add compost, you are adding many microorganisms able to keep the balance of health in the soil. The compost contains natural organisms that will work to the benefit of the soil. It brings in healthy insects while creating a scenario for bad pests to be removed. An example of how this works is the average bird. A natural lawn attracts birds to it, and the birds harvest the pests that should not be in the soil. Thus, the bird is helping improve the overall quality of the soil.

Consider the type of pests you have and then determine what the best treatment option is. The simplest way to learn what type of pests you have is to take a sample of the soil or to just get down on grass level and look. If you are unsure of the type of pest, the University of Minnesota offers an online identification tool at **www.extension.umn.edu/distribution/horticulture/DG1008. html**. One type of biological control is the use of Bt, or bacillus thuringiensis. This product is something you can find online at websites such as Home Harvest® (**http://homeharvest.com**). Purchase it to help control caterpillars, moths, and similar types of pests in the lawn.

Botanical controls

Botanical controls are often the last solution to consider. Use these after you have exhausted all other methods listed here first.

Botanical controls are plant-based control methods sold in garden centers as organic or natural solutions for dealing with pests.

These plant-based treatments can be effective, but use them with limits. Although they are plant based, this does not mean they are safe for humans or pets. In addition, not all products are 100 percent organic — this is what you want to look for. They are often soaps or oils that can have side effects when humans come into contact with them. Some options to consider include boric acid, citrus oils, copper, sulfur, compost teas, and diatomaceous earth. Home Harvest sells many of these, but a knowledgeable local garden center can also help.

Fighting Pests by Species

Thousands of species of insects and other pests lurk throughout lawns across the country and around the world. It would be impractical to list them all here with treatment solutions. In many cases, people need to deal with only a handful of pests on a regular basis, and those are included here.

Armyworms

Armyworms, which are the larval form of moths, chew down turf grasses and are major pests in Southern lawns. Although it is difficult to predict when an armyworm outbreak will occur, they seem to become a problem after the fall rain arrives. You will be able to detect armyworm damage if you have areas of lawn where the grass seems unusually colored and eventually turns brown as the damage worsens. Natural predators, such as ground beetles, skunks, and other rodents, will help reduce armyworm damage, but you may also purchase a bacillus thuringiensis insecticide to help combat this problem.

Black ant

The black ant is one of the most common and most difficult to treat of the pests in lawns. People do not like ants, but black ants

in lawns do little damage to the soil or to the grass. You may not want them in your home, but you will not find a problem with them in your lawn.

These pests are actually highly beneficial to the lawn because they create tunnels for grass to grow in. These ants also place their eggs and search for food sources within these tunnels. If you do wish to reduce the number of black ants in your lawn, do so using physical methods. Rake out any anthills you see. You can also add boiling water over the top of these hills to get rid of the ants. Boric acid will work to get rid of the ants as a botanical control.

Chiggers

Chiggers, also known as red bugs, are common in lawns near wooded or surrounding grassy areas. They crawl onto plants and wait to attach to a host, which can be snakes, toads, birds, rodents, other animals, and sometimes humans as accidental hosts. The best way to naturally prevent against chiggers is to mow lawns and remove unnecessary shrubs or weeds that host the pests.

Chinch bugs

Another culprit lurking in some lawns is the chinch bug. It is a black and white bug in adult form. This type of bug can damage the grass. You may notice a yellowing of the blades that occurs when these insects bite the blades to suck moisture. If you notice this, you will want to apply cultural controls to the lawn. One option is to heavily water the lawn because these bugs do best in droughts. It is also possible to raise the mower blade by an inch and to cut the grass less frequently. Leave grass clippings on the lawn because this makes it harder for the bugs to get the sunlight they need. You can also apply more nitrogen to the soil during the fall treatment to ensure a nitrogen-rich soil, which deters these pests.

Mole crickets

Another bug many American lawns deal with is the mole cricket. This bug is about 1½ inches long and looks much like a traditional cricket with a larger head. These bugs eat grass roots, but they also create significant tunnels under these roots to a point where too much of the soil is removed from the grass roots. You may notice these holes are large enough to put your finger into. The lawn feels spongy when walking on it, too.

Cricket in front of his hole.

If you have mole crickets, it is a good idea to use biological controls because no physical or cultural treatments are effective. Instead, apply nematodes in the early spring, just as the soil begins to warm. You may also find botanical controls available specifically to deal with mole crickets.

Sod webworms

Photo courtesy of The Connecticut Agricultural Experiment Station

When mowing the lawn during the springtime, especially in the evening, you may notice small moths that come out of the lawn. This is the adult form of the sod webworms. At this time, they are dropping eggs that will later create a bad situation in your lawn if you allow them to hatch. These eggs are problematic because they will lead to a larger infestation. You may see dead grass when this infestation reaches its highest point.

A natural control for this type of bug is simply to create a well-balanced soil. You will want to dethatch the grass properly as this will remove much of the area where these pests like to hide and breed. In addition to this, you may find that other critters are more than willing to help control this population for you. Birds, ants, and beetles all feast on these bugs, so if the soil is well balanced, you may not need to take action to correct them. If you do decide to correct this pest problem, you will need to use the botanical controls Bt or pyrethrin as a last resort.

Sow bugs

These insects are known by many names, such as wood louse, armadillo bug, and slater. These are not, in fact, an insect but are related to the shrimp family and hide under compost, organic debris, logs, and any damp place. They have six pairs of legs and a series of armor plates rippling along their back that allows them to curl up into a small ball as their defense system. They are brown and can grow up to a ½ inch long. They feed on all types of young plants and young, newly emerged seedlings, as well as decaying matter. The toad is a helpful predator of the sow bug.

White grubs

White grubs are any type of beetle in their larval stage. These are white in color and have a yellow head. These pests can eat at the roots of your grass, and they can also tunnel significantly. In some cases, their presence will attract other unwanted pests, including moles and skunks, that will dig up your lawn to find them.

The best type of control here is the use of biological controls. Use **milky spore** or **nematodes** to help control white grubs. Milky spore is a type of bacteria that lives in soil, and nematodes are a type of worm that is beneficial to the soil. Only use these treatments if the infestation becomes significant and you have a great deal of damage to the lawn as a result. These treatment options can be expensive, and they can require several applications.

Fungal Infestations

Another type of pest less commonly thought of as a pest and more of a disease is the fungal variety. Several types of fungal conditions can invade your lawn and cause various problems. Some of the most common are listed here. Treat these as you would any other pest problem.

Brown patches

Brown patches are one of the more common fungal conditions. This condition is most commonly caused by having too much water on the lawn. The patches are a circular shape, and if the weather is hot and humid, the conditions are ideal for brown patches to occur.

You can treat this by allowing the grass to dry out so the first inch or so of the lawn is dry. Then, improve the soil conditions by dethatching the soil, aerating it, and improving its overall drainage of water. This often handles the underlying fungal problem because it removes the moisture that remains on the surface of the plants, thus not allowing fungus to grow there.

Dollar spot

In spring and fall, a condition known as dollar spot is likely to occur if your lawn remains moist for too long. This condition occurs because there is heavy thatch on the soil and in the grass and also because you may have a nitrogen deficiency in the lawn. Dollar spot looks like you bleached the area. If you get up close to the grass, you may notice white, cotton-like threads of fungus on the blades. This is a fungal condition you need to control.

To do so, do not immediately use fungicide products. Instead, first improve water drainage on the lawn. You also need to focus on improving the soil's health by adding more nitrogen or compost to the lawn. In addition to this, you may need to seed the lawn using a grass seed that is more disease resistant than what you are currently using. Allow the lawn to dry out before you water it again to ensure you do not have too much water on the lawn for too long of a time.

Those Bigger Pests

Pests, such as moles, can really get into your lawn and do some damage. These critters, though larger than other pests present in your lawn, are often harder to treat because they lurk in the yard in the middle of the night. These creatures see your lawn

Mole.

as food for them, including the grass itself and the grubs lurking in the grass. In most cases, you do not want to ruin your grass quality to get rid of moles or voles, but you can improve the insect levels to reduce the number of pests drawn to the soil.

Take steps to reduce the number of pests in your lawn as described previously, especially if you have a significant infestation. A large infestation is having six or more grubs per square foot of your lawn. You can test this by simply looking at the grass close up. Break up the soil, and look at how many critters lurk in it. If you have too many, apply the appropriate type of treatment for those grubs as recommended.

Fresh molehill or mole mound.

In most cases, these bigger pests will go away if you get rid of the grubs. If they do not, you can try to catch them using traps from a home improvement center, or a better option is to contact an exterminator. On the other hand, you can simply let them be and fix the soil after each of their excursions into your yard.

Taking steps to improve the condition of your lawn means taking the time to get rid of pests and to handle weeds properly. The good news is that a healthy lawn will naturally deter these problems to a level where you simply do not need to take additional steps. One of the ways you can minimize the risks to your lawn is to simply focus on good mowing habits. *There is a process to successfully mowing your lawn, as you will see in the next chapter.*

Chapter 11

MOWING YOUR LAWN THE RIGHT WAY

Mowing seems like a simple thing. All you need to do is to turn on the lawn mower and go up and down the lawn until it is cut, right? Unfortunately, there is more to the process than that, though mowing does not have to be complex. Mowing is a vital process for lawn care in a natural lawn. Specifically, you need to use mowing as a way to help you to achieve the lawn you are looking for.

Consider the act of mowing. Mowing the lawn means that you are taking off a significant portion of a plant and assuming it will grow back healthy. Cutting into a plant like this, as with any type of plant, can cause harm if done improperly. Cutting the grass is an unnatural act in itself. In nature, no one mows the grass down, but instead it grows, seeds, dies, and then becomes compost for new plants. Even though cutting your lawns is something you can and should do, you need to do so in the right manner to have a healthy lawn.

If you cut a lawn improperly, you leave the grass vulnerable to health concerns. When you remove the top portion of a grass blade, the lawn is more susceptible to the various conditions surrounding it, which is when fungal conditions, weeds, and insects can damage the lawn. To mow your lawn correctly, you will need to do two things. First, you need to focus on having a healthy lawn as this book encourages. By maintaining healthy soil, keeping pests under control, and handling weeds effectively, you prevent mowing from damaging the lawn. The second element is decreasing the amount of time it takes for the lawn to heal and recover itself after a mowing. Mowing at the right height, for example, ensures the blades of grass will be long enough for the plant to obtain the necessary sunlight it needs.

Should you leave the mowing to a professional? Many people have professional landscapers come in to mow their lawn, even after investing a great deal of time and money into maintaining a natural lawn. The benefit of doing this is that with the right company, you can create a healthy lawn that meets all of your particular needs without having to worry about mowing. The catch is, though, that you need to ensure the mowing company you select will apply the natural techniques you will learn in this chapter. Not all companies will do this, but others specialize in it. To find a landscaping company in your area, simply ask companies if they offer this type of care. You can find companies in your Yellow Pages, or some may have websites. Ask the company if it uses organic fertilizers or provides maintenance techniques that are less damaging to grass. Find out how flexible the company is to meet your organic lawn care goals.

Mowing your own lawn is more beneficial to the lawn and to you because you get to see the lawn up close as you work through the process. This means you are more likely to spot problems occurring at their initial phases so you can remedy them before they get out of hand. Dead spots, pest problems, and even weeds mowed over by a contractor may hide problems from your view. Keep in mind that the key to a successful, natural lawn is to learn what your lawn needs from the signs it offers you.

Taking that into consideration, you need to take a few steps as you mow your lawn to ensure you give the lawn the best possible opportunity to remain healthy.

Mowing Tips

In order to have a healthy, good-looking lawn, incorporate a few good mowing techniques. When you mow your lawn using these methods, you will see the difference.

One of the first things you need to do is to check the mower itself. In Chapter 5, you learned how to choose a mower for your lawn. Just because you have a lawn mower does not mean it is ready to go as soon as you turn it on. Make sure to check the mower's blade at least once a month to ensure it is sharp. You also need to tune up the mower as often as the manufacturer's warranty guidelines state. If you do not have an owner's manual, check the manufacturer's website for a copy. Apply the techniques for maintaining the mower as recommended by the manufacturer to keep it functioning properly and to ensure the lawn does not suffer as a result of the machinery's poor performance.

Before you begin mowing, check the oil and fuel levels. Do this on the pavement rather than the grass to avoid spilling gasoline onto the grass, which will kill it. You also want to look underneath the mower into the undercarriage to ensure no grass or other debris is lodged in it. Do this every time you mow to ensure the lawn mower works properly.

Next, look at your lawn itself. Walk over the surface of the lawn, and pick up anything in the grass that should not be there. Toys, sticks, hoses, and other debris need removal to ensure they do not damage the mower or you by flying back at you if you mow over the top of it. In addition, feel the ground. How wet is it? It is not a good idea to mow the lawn when it feels wet to the touch because mowing a wet lawn damages the turf and the grass. Check the overall height of the lawn. Some areas of your lawn may grow faster than others do, such as in areas where water drains into a basin or where there is more sun.

The best time of the day to head out to mow is in the early evening because the sun and heat levels should be lower during this time than during the day. The grass does not have dew on it, as it does in the morning, which makes it an ideal time to mow the lawn. Avoid mowing in the middle of the day when the blaring sun could damage the grass's ability to recovery from the mow.

Also, there are times when you should not mow at all. If the grass is only starting to get tall and your rain levels have been low, avoid mowing. Mowing the lawn stimulates the grass to grow, which requires more water. If you do not expect rain for several days, do not mow. Tall grass can withstand a short or long drought more effectively than shorter grasses trying to grow.

Should you mow now?

When should you mow your organic lawn? Mow when the grass height reaches the level appropriate for cutting, which differs based on the type of lawn you have. If you are using bent grass, Bermuda grass, or similar types, you can mow the lawn 1 inch or lower. Most other grasses need to be taller to survive properly after the mowing occurs. Mowing to a height of about 2 inches is the standard accepted level.

In addition to this, realize that you may need to adjust your mowing frequency based on the time of year. In the summer months, the high heat levels mean the grass is likely to grow at a much slower rate, so you will not need to mow as often. In the spring, when the grass grows at its fastest rate, you can mow the grass when it reaches 1½ inches tall. In the fall, the grass needs to grab as many nutrients it can to overwinter properly. At this time of the year, mow the lawn no shorter than 2 inches.

The actual mowing process

Now that you know when to mow and how to prepare to mow, the next step is putting the mower on the lawn and getting to it. Your house is your guide as to where to start mowing. You will want to vary where you start and the direction of the mow each time you mow to ensure all grass blades have the ability to grow properly. Look for lines on your home, such as the line forming the wall of your home, to help you with this process. For example, select a line parallel to the house or one that runs perpendicular to the house. You can go on the diagonal of the house, too. Varying the direction of your mowing pattern helps prevent the grass from compacting under the mower wheels, as it does when you mow in the same direction time and time again.

Do not mow the lawn in a circle. This offers no consistency for the lawn and it is not a natural motion for the lawn mower. As such, it will cause more damage of the lawn. It is also harder to do and wastes your energy.

As you begin to mow, complete the first line in a straight line. Then, turn around to come back up in the opposite direction. When doing this, overlap the second line over the top of the previous line's tire marks by about 2 inches. As you make that turn, be sure to pick up the top portion of the mower as you turn to avoid cutting the grass too low as you turn the mower. For those using an electric mower, it is critical to ensure the cord always remains behind you throughout the process to avoid running it over.

As you work through the lawn, always push the lawn mower forward. Avoid pulling it back toward you. Most mulching mowers do their job best when they move in a forward direction. This process allows the mower to cut, mulch, and then disperse the lawn clippings properly. Some types of mowers, including reel varieties, will not cut at all when you pull back on them. It is also not safe to pull a mower back toward you because the blade continues to turn and can run over your feet. Read the manufacturer's guide to your lawn mower to ensure you do not jeopardize your safety when using this device.

To bag or not to bag is a question many people ask. A few times a year, it is acceptable to mow the lawn using a bag attachment. Most times of the year, mow without it. Mulching the clippings back into the lawn provides the soil with the nutrition derived from this organic matter. It also helps with water retention and providing shade for the grass from the sun.

One time when you should use a bag attachment is at the beginning of the season when you mow the lawn for the first time. The bag attachment will help pick up all of the dead grass and some of the thatch material. Another instance when you should use the bag attachment is when the lawn has weeds going to seed such as when you notice dandelions forming. Mowing the lawn with the attachment will help grab most of those seeds and allow you to dispose of them in another area outside of your lawn's grass. Another instance to use the bag attachment is when there are a large number of leaves on the grass. If you have just a few trees, you can mulch this material into the lawn as an organic fertilizer. In cases where you have numerous leaves, mulching it in will do more harm than good. Use a bag attachment, and make sure to add this material to your compost bin.

Mowing problems

There are some instances when you could make simple mistakes that have drastic effects on your lawn. One of them is cutting too much at one time in situations where the lawn has gotten significantly taller than it should. If you went on vacation or you were too busy to get to the grass this week, you may feel tempted to simply cut the grass down to the normal level and get done with the process. However, this catch-up method will damage your lawn. Never cut more than one-third of the grass's height at one time because doing so limits the grass's ability to recover from the mowing. In situations like this, you need to come back and cut the grass a second time, or until you reach its normal level. Be sure to leave at least two days in between mows to ensure the lawn can recover enough from the process.

Another common problem with mowing is **scalping**, which occurs when you cut the grass so low that you can see the soil underneath. This often happens when the mower slips or otherwise goes off course and cuts the grass at a length too low. This normally happens accidently. It can also happen if you use a string trimmer along the edge of the lawn and get too low to the ground. The best way to avoid this is to be aware of instances when the wheels of the mower can get too low. If it does happen, you may need to re-seed the area if it does not grow back.

By following these steps, you will be well on your way to creating a healthy lawn that looks great. If you find yourself unable to get to a level where you mow consistently, it may be best to hire a professional to handle the mowing. Properly mowing your lawn improves its health.

Edging Your Lawn Properly

Edging your lawn is an important part of creating an aesthetically appealing lawn. It is, for the most part, the same process as cutting the grass except that you are using a handheld trimmer. Before you can do that, though, you need to get an edge in place. You may like straight lines and even edges throughout your yard, or you may like curved lines that form unique garden beds. In all circumstances, it takes a few hours of hard work to get them in place. Once you establish your edges and maintain them, you will have a beautiful edge line created around your flowerbeds and pathways.

All you need to do is to take a hoe to the lawn. Craft out the shape you like using the hoe. There are no rules here; the goal is to find a look you like. It does not have to follow the shape of your home. On the other hand, you can create an edge that runs along your house in a straight line. Cut about 2 to 3 inches in depth. You can invest in an edger to do this for you, but these can be expensive and require fossil fuels to work. You get the best-finished product with a hoe or spade.

Once you have the shape cut out, create your garden bed using whatever materials you like. Your lawn remains the same. The question is, what are you going to put in the space you cut out? Many people still use edging materials such as blocks or aluminum fencing products. If you like this, there is no reason not to use them. Simply install them and maintain them. Many other people are turning to creating a natural look. In either case, you will need to use a trimmer to cut back the grass along the edge each time you cut the grass. But, avoid letting the lower wheel mow in this area because it will scalp the grass along the edge.

You may need to come back to these landscaped borders every few months to cut them out again to get that clean line. If you do not want this amount of work on a regular basis, the best option for you is to install permanent edge material, such as brick, plastic, wood, or other materials.

Consider edging and trimming as important as cutting the grass, to the extent that you want to maintain the overall height of the grass along this edge to match the rest of your lawn.

Removing Thatch

Two misconceptions out there are that grass clippings lead to thatch or that you do not need to remove thatch. Grass clippings and thatch are different, and you need to take action to remove thatch from your lawn frequently. Clippings are not thatch.

Thatch is dead grass that has roots still in place. This creates a layer of dead material between the soil and the green grass growing above it. As you leave thatch in place, a thick layer will develop, which if left in place will block the soil from water, sunlight, and air circulation, all important elements in maintaining the health of the lawn.

Where does thatch come from then? A product in the grass's roots called lignin leads to the development of thatch. Lignin does not decompose as fast as other plant material. As such, the slow decomposition process leads to thatch development. If that is the case, why do grass clippings easily decompose when this root does not? The grass clippings you remove, assuming you remove only the top third of the grass blade, are 90 percent water. Once you cut the blades, they decompose right away, and most do not last more than a few days before they are virtually gone.

Thatch can develop faster in lawns built on a synthetic system because of the higher level of nitrogen in the soil these lawns have. The nitrogen levels in the soil enable green shoots of grass to grow quickly, and this pushes them up out of the soil while creating a lifeless soil. This further slows the decomposition of the dead plant's grass roots.

It is normal to have some level of thatch in a lawn, even a fully organic lawn, because it is part of the life cycle of the grass itself. In a lawn that has a healthy soil composition, there will be less thatch occurring. The microorganisms found within the soil will help speed up the process of decomposing this material. In addition, the topical treatments of compost tea you add, which contain high levels of microorganisms, also feast on the thatch, breaking it down further. For this reason, you never get an excessive buildup of thatch.

If you do have a significant amount of thatch or you are just starting the season, you will need to rake through the lawn to remove it. Use a bamboo rake to gather the thatch out of the lawn. Then, remove it from the lawn altogether, and place into a compost bin.

Keep the clippings

Unlike thatch, grass clippings should remain in your soil. By simply mulching them into the lawn using your mower, you return about half of the lawn's annual nitrogen needs. A worrisome fact from the EPA states that yard waste, such as grass clippings, accounts for the second most commonly found product in solid waste material placed in the trash. The first most common item is paper. Yet, both are recyclable. As such, many communities have moved to a system that does not allow refuse collectors to remove these types of yard waste in the general refuse collection, though some communities offer secondary recycling pickups that may take yard waste. If your community does not pick up this type of waste, compost the quality grass clippings or use the clippings as mulch. Check with your community refuse department to learn if this is the case within your community.

What happens when the clippings are just too thick to leave on the lawn? This can happen if the lawn is overseeded or in situations where you have let the grass grow too high — even cutting it a few days apart may still result in a significant amount of grass clippings on the lawn. In these situations, it is best to simply rake up the excessive grass clippings. After this is done, you can add the clippings directly to your compost bin.

Do not attempt to leave these clippings in place. Excessive clippings can make it difficult for the grass to get enough sunlight and water, which can kill the grass. After mowing the grass, if you can obviously see the grass clippings, you may need to rake them up. Make sure to add them as fertilizer to your lawn for the best overall effect.

Maintaining your lawn with these ideal mowing methods will make a significant difference in the overall look and health of it. Be consistent in your care of the lawn to see the results you want.

Chapter 12

GOING FOR LESS LAWN

$\mathcal{I}$n a natural setting, grass does not have as much of an opportunity to prosper as it does in today's American lawn, especially when homeowners use organic methods such as the ones mentioned in this book to create a natural lawn. In a natural setting, the landscape has a variety of plants of numerous species. All live together to create a cohesive ecosystem that supports itself. Even while incorporating a natural lawn, there is no way to create a self-sustaining lawn similar to what occurs in a natural setting. The gardener will always have to adjust soil, mow the lawn, and handle weeds.

Creating a beautiful lawn does not mean you have to focus solely on using grass. In many cases, incorporating other natural substances, plants, and a variety features creates a more interesting and appealing landscape than the traditional lawn on its own. Another benefit to incorporating more of these additional features into the lawn is you can easily cut down on the amount of space needed for an actual lawn. For those who have less time to focus on an organic lawn and who are looking for something lower in maintenance, consider going for the less lawn look.

There are simple ways to limit the amount of grass in your yard, including using trees and shrubs. There are also additional ways to change out the look of a solid patch of green grass with ornamental grasses, rock gardens, and even water features. In this chapter, you will learn some of the ways you can limit the overall amount of grass you need to manage and create areas of your lawn that add more interest and appeal.

First, consider the amount of space you want to take away from the lawn itself and the condition of the lawn. If you have an area that is virtually untouched, leave it that way. Having a completely natural area could be one of the best features of your yard. If this is the route you take, make sure none of the weeds or other invasive species are present that could otherwise ruin the natural elements of the lawn.

In other cases, you may have a lawn with more planning and structure and you want to add something different or enhance know that all of the steps you have taken to improve the overall health of your lawn remain vital here. You do not want to add or do anything to the soil and the plants already present that would incorporate any synthetic products. Your goal is to have a totally organic landscape.

Types of Additions to Your Lawn

If you have an area of your lawn where you want to implement something different, what are your options? A good place to start is with grass, but other options are available that do not require a weekly time investment.

Ornamental grasses are those that look like overgrown grasses that reach significant heights, such as the maiden grass cultivators huron brush and huron sentinel. Homeowners use these grasses for aesthetics rather than creating an entire lawn. Most varieties are low maintenance. Once you plant them, you do not need to do much with them besides provide water when the climate becomes too dry. You also need to cut them back in the fall so they can conserve energy to overwinter. Another option to consider is the no-mow grass. If you are someone who wants the look of the lawn but does not want the actual work of mowing, then a no-mow grass can be the ideal investment. These grasses grow much like a traditional grass, but they do not grow above a certain height, which varies according to species. Some species of no-mow grass are fox trot and red head. In most cases, they do not grow more than a few inches in height and require no real mowing. This type of grass does best in cooler climates, such as the Northeast or upper Midwest.

Another option to consider is ground cover. As the name implies, this type of lawn is made up of a plant life that clings to the actual ground rather than expanding upward. You can walk on them similar to what you do with a lawn, but they require far less maintenance than your average lawn does. You can incorporate any of the native ground covers in your area into your lawn. To create a visually appealing space, consider investing in more than one type. Use a mixture of perennials, vines, and shrubs here. Choose from a variety of types of ground covers, including various colors and shapes, to create a visually appealing space. Plant options here include pachysandra procumbens, Isotoma fluviatilis, and ajuga reptans. Consider using any type of fern, too. Species such as maidenhair and bird's nest work well.

The rain garden

Ornamental grasses are fantastic, but they may not be what you are looking for. If you are hoping for something a bit less hands-on or more unique, consider using a rain garden. A **rain garden** is a type of landscape that allows excess water to drain properly into the soil naturally. If your land sits at the bottom of a hill where water easily gathers after a rain, this is an ideal investment for you. People build these rain gardens to help utilize the excess rain that can build up in these areas.

If you are looking for a reason to build a rain garden, consider any of following benefits of using this type of garden:

- Rain gardens help replenish groundwater supplies.

- They work to increase the amount of wildlife and natural insect population to healthy levels.

- They reduce the amount of pollutants that make it to the lakes and rivers.

- Rain gardens also help reduce the amount of standing water your lawn may have.

How can you incorporate this type of landscape? Choose a sunny area of the yard at least 10 feet from your home. You do not want it near a septic system. After it rains, watch the way the water moves, normally down a hill or next to a hard surface. This area where rain travels naturally is where you want to target. Once you select a location, plan to direct water to the location from downspouts or other areas of the yard where it is possible to do so.

Once you have done this, the next step is to select the right plants for the area. Focus on plants that will tolerate some level of drought but that like moist soil. If you wish to be completely natural here, the good thing to do is to select plants native to your area.

You will need to dig out the area to remove any grass or other plants living there. Then, prepare the soil using the techniques listed throughout this book. A well-balanced soil should be loose and full of organic matter. Once you fill in the plants in the garden, you can allow this area to grow without a lot of focus on maintaining it. Keep in mind that you can select the position of plants and the overall shape, design, and look of the space. There are no rules.

More Options to Consider

Are you still looking for something interesting and unique to incorporate into this space? Consider using a flower meadow. Although people have gotten away from this particular type of landscaping, instead choosing the more modern, crisp, spacious lawn of sprawling grass, it can be visually appealing to see wildflowers growing in the dense grass. In fact, in order to accomplish this type of gardenscape, you only need to stop cutting the grass and avoid using any type of synthetic products on the lawn. Within a short time, you will see a variety of beautiful flowers springing forth because flower meadows grow quickly and without much attention. Seeding the area will produce flowers faster, but in most areas, a natural flowering meadow will occur. You can also introduce a range of different flowers into the garden meadow and allow them to take hold naturally. Keep in mind this type of garden can invite larger pests into the area, including mice and moles.

If you do not want to include flowers but want a harder surface, consider a rock garden. With the proper foundation, which includes quality soil content, you can create a rock garden that requires little attention from you on a regular basis. This type of garden can incorporate some of the ground cover mentioned previously, or it can be strictly rocks. Many people focus on allowing it to grow itself, assuming there are no invasive weeds lurking in the garden. This creates a natural landscape you can be happy with having as a yard.

It is also possible to create a healthy lawn that is right for you with the right combination of plants, grasses, and other mediums throughout the growing space. The key to growing an organic lawn is to make it your own unique space that uses simple and natural applications to keep the lawn healthy. The good news is that the rules are not as tight as you might think.

Conclusion

Creating an organic lawn can be a rewarding experience. There are plenty of instances when it is going to be challenging, especially when those weeds just keep showing up. The good news is it is all worth the hard work. If you have worked your way through this book, you now know the risks of using synthetic products on lawns, and even though many companies would like us to believe it, these products are not good for humans, pets, or the lawn itself. Although modern science plays catch-up to the natural processes in the earth, stay focused on developing an all-natural lawn you are proud of calling your own. Many people will spend a small fortune on pesticides and other chemical-based products, but you will not. Instead, you will focus on creating a natural environment for the soil to thrive in so plants, including your lawn, can be beautiful and lush.

Is it Worth the Work?

Look out of your window right now. Do you see a lawn you know is healthy? If you did not apply a chemical-based fertilizer this year, would the lawn look awful within a few months? Most likely so, if your lawn is not yet converted to an organic lawn.

You will likely spend hundreds of dollars each year in combined expenses to care for your lawn, including the fertilizers you will have to put down, the chemicals to treat weeds, the insect killers, and the products to overseed the lawn. Instead of doing all of that work to create a lawn that depends on you to survive, create a lawn that requires less dependency and ensures the earth remains safe and protected. The initial work of creating a natural lawn is a bit more challenging, but once you have done that work, it takes far fewer steps to maintain. As you keep that in mind, remember that you are also doing something amazing for the earth as well: You are protecting the earth from chemicals.

Enjoy your lawn. After you work through the steps in this book, take a step back and realize that you have accomplished a feat not many people do. What you can do now is enjoy it.

Allow your kids to run and play games on your lawn. Allow your pets to sniff out the lurking pests. Spend time enjoying conversations with your family while relaxing in the yard. You can and should take advantage of all of your hard work. After all, you have created an ecosystem that depends less on you and on synthetic products. In addition to that, the ecosystem in your lawn can withstand many of the harshest weather conditions and even damage from invaders.

For many people, the goal of a natural lawn is achievable. In order to get to that point, roll up your sleeves and begin the hard work. Then, make sure to tell your neighbors all that you have accomplished to encourage them to do the same. You could change the world, at least a little bit.

Appendix A

COMMERCIAL ORGANIC HERBICIDES

Organic Herbicide

Product Name	Active Ingredient	Purpose
All Down Organic Weed Killer	Citric acid, garlic	Kills unwanted grass and weeds
Ground Force Organic Herbicide	Citric acid, garlic extract	Used to kill all vegetation
Burn Out II	Clove oil, vinegar, lemon juices	Kills unwanted weeds and grass
Everything Must Go	Citric acid, garlic extract, lauryl sulfate	Total vegetation control
Corn gluten meal	Corn starch	Weed suppressant and lawn fertilizer
Garden Weasel Crabgrass Killer	Cinnamon bark	Crabgrass and weed killer
Weed Zap	Cinnamon oil, clove oil	Kills unwanted grass and weeds; does not differentiate

REFERENCE GUIDE FOR ORGANIC LAWN CARE THROUGHOUT THE YEAR

Time of year	What to Do	Pests	Soil Additives
February to early March Dormant grass	Sharpen mower blades and test your soil		Apply nothing at this time
March 15 to April 15 Roots begin to grow	Remove winter debris, dethatch if thatch is greater than ½ inch, overseed weedy and thin areas	Suppress weed germination with corn gluten, apply just before forsythia blooms	Use corn gluten as a high nitrogen fertilizer

Time of year	What to Do	Pests	Soil Additives
April 15 to June 15 Shoots grow rapidly and roots grow slowly, lots of use of carbohydrates to promote leaf growth	Overseed weedy and thin areas, aerate, add soil nutrients, begin mowing	Pull dandelions out by hand, suppress crabgrass by mowing high	Use soil test and apply nutrients, minerals and lime as indicated, apply compost if necessary
June 15 to Aug. 15 Shoot and root growth is slow, grass is susceptible to insects and to damage from foot traffic	Continue to mow at 3-inch height, apply compost tea	Use nematodes to control white grubs, use compost tea to aid in prevention of weeds, insects, and disease	Apply compost tea every two weeks
Aug. 15 to Sept. 15 Shoot and root growth increases as temperature drops	Continue cutting at 3 inches, re-seed thin areas, seed new lawn areas, apply organic fertilizer		Apply organic fertilizer as recommended from spring testing
Sept. 15 to Nov. 1 Slow shoot growth, but active root growth	Shred and remove leaves, aerate lawn, last mowing		Apply lime as necessary, leave shredded leaves to apply vital nutrients
November to February Grass is dormant	Plan next year's garden and enjoy not having to care for the lawn		Apply nothing now

Appendix C

HOMEMADE ORGANIC PESTICIDES

This section describes some of the mixtures you can create at home and apply to your lawn. All these mixtures are more natural than the synthetic options available and can be made with items commonly found around the home.

Soapy Spray

This mixture is great if you have slugs crawling through your lawn. To create this mixture, add 3 tablespoons of liquid organic dish detergent into 1 gallon of water. Mix well, and spray on affected areas once a week.

Garlic Spray

This is another spray you can use if you have slugs in your lawn. To make this spray, you will need one garlic bulb, 1 quart of water, one medium onion, 1 tablespoon cayenne pepper, and 1 tablespoon organic liquid dish soap.

Crush the garlic, and mince it finely. Add finely chopped onion to the garlic mixture, and add the rest of the ingredients except the soap. Wait one hour, and then add soap to the mixture. The ingredients must steep, similar to a tea. After you add the soap, the mixture is ready to use. You can store this spray in the fridge for one week.

Buttermilk and Flour Spray

Use this spray to rid your lawn of cutworms, wireworms, whiteflies, and slugs. You will need 1 pint of water, 2 teaspoons of paraffin, ¼ cup organic dish liquid, and 6 tablespoons chopped garlic. To make the spray, soak the whole garlic in liquid paraffin for 24 hours. After 24 hours has gone by, add water and dish liquid to mixture, and shake well. Strain the liquid, and store it in a glass jar. This solution should last approximately seven days.

Hot and Sweet Pepper Spray

This mixture can be used as an all-purpose insecticide for your lawn. Be careful when handling the peppers so you do not accidentally get the mixture into your eyes. Also exercise caution if using this mixture around children.

To create this mixture, combine ½ cup fresh spearmint, ½ cup hot red peppers, ½ cup horseradish roots and leaves, 2 tablespoons liquid dish detergent, ½ cup green onion tops, and water. Mix horseradish, spearmint leaves, peppers, and onion tops together with enough water to cover the mixture. Strain the mixture and add ½ gallon of water and detergent. To use this solution on your lawn, mix ½ gallon of the solution with ½ gallon of water. This spray will keep for a few days in a cool location.

HOMEMADE ORGANIC HERBICIDES

The following are some natural remedies you can use to rid your lawn of pesky weeds and unwanted plants.

Citrus Vinegar Solution

To create this mixture, you will need 1 gallon of vinegar, ¼ cup orange oil, 2 tablespoons dish detergent, and 1 cup lemon juice concentrate. Combine the dish detergent, vinegar, lemon juice, and orange oil in a large bowl. Stir the ingredients well and pour into a spray bottle. Spray the mixture on the affected areas until saturated, making sure to apply some of the mixture to the ground to kill the roots. Reapply as needed to kill weed growth.

Adding some of the following elements to your lawn will also help get rid of unwanted plants. Be warned that adding some of these items might also lead to all plants growing in the area, not just weeds, to die.

- **Vinegar:** Vinegar removes moisture, and when sprayed on plants, draws water out of them. Vinegar may either only dry out the top growth of the plant or may seep down into the roots and dry them out as well, depending on the plant and how mature it is. It may also dry out and kill your lawn, so exercise caution when applying to your grass.

- **Boiling water:** Adding plain, boiling water to weeds should be enough to kill them but will also kill the grass nearby the application site. To better control where the water is added to the lawn, bring water to a boil in a tea pot, and pour onto weeds. This effectively cooks the plant, thereby killing it.

Glossary

Adsorbents: substances that collect a liquid, gas, or dissolved substance on their surfaces

Black water: water that comes from sewers, kitchen sinks, and dishwashers and is not recommended for use on lawns

Bubblers: small sprinkler heads that dispense water at a slow rate and for a small area as opposed to a large garden

Coenzyme factor: a substance that needs to be present along with an enzyme so a certain reaction can take place

Compost tea: a liquid version of compost

Cultural solution: finding a way to treat a pest problem using a method that is safe and similar to some of the steps taken to prevent weeds

Dethatch: removing all the dead materials from the lawn

Drip irrigation: applying water directly to the roots of the plant in a slow dripping process to allow the water to seep into the soil

Field: an area containing plants that is not mowed on a regular basis

Gray water: water you have used for something in the recent past that can be harvested and reused on the lawn

Humus: organic matter in compost that has finished decaying

Inoculant: a substance that helps prevent the growth and spread of disease

Lawn: an area of land that has grass growing on it and that a person mows

Macronutrients: substances, such as nitrogen, phosphorus, calcium, sulfur, and magnesium, that plants need in large quantities to grow

Micronutrients: substances, such as iron, manganese, zinc, copper, molybdenum, boron, and chlorine, that plants need in small quantities to grow

Milky spores: a type of bacteria that lives in the soil

Necrosis: a condition associated with excess fluoride in water used on grass that burns grass, causing the tips of the blades of grass to turn yellow

Nematodes: a type of worm that is beneficial to the soil

Nontoxic: substances that are safe to touch with bare hands that will not harm the body of a human or an animal that comes in contact with it

Organic lawn care: the practice of creating and maintaining the health and well being of a lawn using natural or organic practices as opposed to artificial substances

Organic: any natural substance derived from an animal, plant, or mineral source

Overseeding: adding more seeds to an existing lawn

Pre-emergent control: a method that allows gardeners to get more control over weeds by stopping them from going to seed

Rain garden: a type of landscape that allows excess water to drain properly into the soil in a natural way

Rhizomes: horizontally growing stems that are usually found underground

Scalping: cutting the grass so low that the soil underneath is visible

Soil amendment: something added to soil to boost its organic content

Solarization: placing a flexible black rubber over an area where weeds are growing to allow the sun to bake the covered area and kill the weeds

Sprayers: an irrigation system that sprays water over an entire area, allowing the roots of the plant to maintain optimum soil moisture

Stolons: creeping stems that grow above ground

Thatch: a term used to describe matted grass and nondecaying material that likely prevents fertilizer from getting to the soil and offers insects an ideal place to live

Thermoplastic: a new form of plastic that is highly elastic and flexible

Top dressing: a thin layer of compost added to the top of grass

Topsoil: the top layer of soil on your lawn

Vermicomposting: a form of creating compost using worm castings

Wetting agents: a topical additive for soil that is useful where soil needs more help to absorb and keep water

Winterkills: the process in which poor winter conditions cause damage to grass

Xeriscaping: using grasses and other plants that require less water strategically to reduce the overall water needed

Bibliography

AllDown (**www.alldownherbicide.com**).
Accessed Jan. 3, 2011.

"Bluestem – Little Native Grass Seed." Outsidepride.com
(**www.outsidepride.com/seed/native-grass-seed/bluestem-
little-native-grass-seed.html**). Accessed Jan. 13, 2011.

Davenport, Millie. "Bahia Grass." Clemson Cooperative
Extension (**www.clemson.edu/extension/hgic/pests/weeds/
hgic2316.html**). Accessed Jan. 13, 2011.

Duble, Richard L. "Bermuda Grass." Texas Cooperative
Extension (**http://aggie-horticulture.tamu.edu/archives/
parsons/turf/publications/bermuda.html**).
Accessed Jan. 13, 2011.

Duble, Richard L. "Buffalo Grass." Texas Cooperative Extension (**http://aggie-horticulture.tamu.edu/archives/parsons/turf/publications/buffalo.html**). Accessed Jan. 13, 2011.

Duble, Richard L. "Centipedegrass." Texas Cooperative Extension (**http://aggie-horticulture.tamu.edu/archives/parsons/turf/publications/centipede.html**). Accessed Jan. 13, 2011.

Duble, Richard L. "Kentucky Bluegrass." Texas Cooperative Extension (**http://aggie-horticulture.tamu.edu/archives/parsons/turf/publications/bluegrass.html**). Accessed Jan. 13, 2011.

Duble, Richard L. "St. Augustine Grass." Texas Cooperative Extension (**http://aggie-horticulture.tamu.edu/archives/parsons/turf/publications/staug.html**). Accessed Jan. 13, 2011.

GardenWeb (**www.gardenweb.com**). Accessed Jan. 3, 2011.

GreenCulture (**www.composters.com**). Accessed Jan. 3, 2011.

Home Harvest Garden Supply (**http://homeharvest.com**). Accessed Jan. 3, 2011.

"Homemade Organic Pesticide." eSsortment (**www.essortment.com/all/homemadeorgani_renu.htm**). Accessed Jan. 13, 2011.

Houseman, Richard M. "Chiggers." University of Missouri Extension (**http://extension.missouri.edu/publications/ DisplayPub.aspx?P=g7398**). Accessed Jan. 13, 2011.

Iannotti, Marie. "How Much Mulch?" About.com (**http://gardening.about.com/od/gardenprimer/a/ HowMuchMulch.htm**). Accessed Jan. 3, 2011.

Lowenfels, Jeff, and Wayne Lewis. *Teaming with Microbes: The Organic Gardener's Guide to the Soil Food Web*. Portland, Ore.: Timber, 2010.

Morris, Tracy S. "Homemade Organic Herbicide." Garden Guides (**www.gardenguides.com/119865-homemade-organic-herbicide.html**). Accessed Jan. 13, 2011.

NRCS National Plant Data Center (**http://npdc.usda.gov**). Accessed Jan. 3, 2011.

"Organic Lawn Care For the Cheap and Lazy." Richsoil.com (**www.richsoil.com/lawn-care.jsp**). Accessed Jan. 3, 2011.

Oster, Doug, and Jessica Walliser. *Grow Organic*. Pittsburgh: St. Lynn's Press, 2007.

Rodale Organic Gardening Basics. Emmaus, PA: Rodale, 2000.

Sansone, Chris. "Armyworms in Turfgrass." Texas AgriLife Extension Service (**http://citybugs.tamu.edu/factsheets/ landscape/lawns/ent-1007**). Accessed Jan. 13, 2011.

Tukey, Paul Boardway. *The Organic Lawn Care Manual: A Natural, Low-maintenance System for a Beautiful, Safe Lawn.* North Adams, Mass.: Storey Publishing, 2007.

U.S. Environmental Protection Agency. (**www.epa.gov**). Accessed Jan. 3, 2011.

Whitman, Ann, and Suzanne DeJohn. *Organic Gardening for Dummies.* Hoboken, N.J.: John Wiley & Sons, 2009.

Author Biography

Sandy Baker is a published author of several financial books, including *Your Complete Guide to Early Retirement: A Step-By-Step Plan for Making It Happen* and *The Complete Guide to Planning Your Estate: A Step By Step Plan to Protect Your Assets, Limit Your Taxes, and Ensure Your Wishes Are Fulfilled*. She steps into the world of organic lawn care, a field she is passionate about, in this book.

After years of navigating gardening in a traditional sense, Baker has created a step-by-step process used in her own lawn in Ohio. As an avid fan of healthy environments and taking steps to protect the earth, she studies organic lawn care almost constantly.

Sandy Baker is a mother of three and wife to an ever-supportive husband. She has provided full-time freelance writing for the last six years and writes about topics she finds fascinating.

Index